Parrot
Training

A Guide to Taming and Gentling Your Avian Companion

Parrot Training

A Guide to Taming and Gentling Your Avian Companion

Bonnie Munro Doane

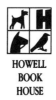

HOWELL
BOOK
HOUSE

Howell Book House

Published by Wiley Publishing, Inc., New York, NY

For general information on our other products and services or to obtain technical support please contact our Customer Care Department within the U.S. at 800-762-2974, outside the U.S. at 317-572-3993 or fax 317-572-4002.

Wiley also publishes its books in a variety of electronic formats. Some content that appears in print may not be available in electronic books.

Library of Congress Cataloging-in-Publication Data:

Doane, Bonnie Munro.
     Parrot training : a guide to taming and gentling your avian companion /
Bonnie Munro Doane ; illustrations by Richard Cole.
     p. cm.
     Rev. ed. of: Pleasure of their company. © 1998.
     ISBN 0-7645-6327-0
     1. Parrots—Training. I. Doane, Bonnie Munro. Pleasure of their company. II. Title.

SF473.P3 D63 2001
636.6'86535—dc21   00-065346

Manufactured in the United States of America
10 9

Book design by A & D Design

In memory of our dearest Mac and for our wonderful J.B.

About the Author

Bonnie Munro Doane, RN, BSN, MSN, has worked with parrots for nearly twenty years. As both a pet owner and breeder, she has broad experience in the areas of parrot behavior and behavioral problems, parrot husbandry, nutrition, breeding and rearing of many species of parrot chicks. For nine years, she held a U.S. Fish and Wildlife Service permit to breed certain endangered parrot species. Ms. Doane has been a member of the Association of Avian Veterinarians since 1987.

Contents

A bundle of feathered joy.

1

Why Train Your Parrot?

A bird has its weight, though a mere feather.

—African proverb

Congratulations! You've just brought home your new parrot.

The chances are it's newly weaned, but perhaps you're still hand-feeding it. You know your little bundle of feathered joy is going to need some pretty consistent tender loving care. Being a good "parrot parent," you're reading everything you can find to help you do your best. You deserve a big pat on the shoulder; indeed, your parrot youngster is a very lucky bird to have you!

This book was written in large part with you and your new friend in mind. You will find much here to help get you off to a good start. It's important for you to know that when you bring your little guy home, it knows how to do only two things: how to trust you, and how not to fear you. Period. Everything else—good, bad, and indifferent—will be learned from you and the other members of your family. You have the sole responsibility for teaching your parrot what it must know to get along happily with its human companions. Without your constant gentle yet firm teaching and guidance, it will revert to the wild ways of its ancestors, and you will both be very unhappy with each other. Your job is that of a

1

parent in many ways. This book is designed to help you parent your parrot in the very most effective way possible.

So read on. Determine to do it correctly from the very beginning, and you'll never regret going the extra mile.

Or . . .

You already have a parrot—and you're in trouble. So is your parrot. You are very disappointed. You need good, practical help, and you need it now. Or who knows how things might end up?

You probably paid a great deal of money for your feathered problem, although at the time you didn't expect any difficulties. Your spending didn't stop there, however. An attractive cage in which your new pet could reside comfortably, as well as its toys and treats, meant dropping yet another bundle to become a parrot owner.

You may have bought your parrot from a pet store. Unless you were very fortunate, the people at the pet store really didn't tell you very much about how to care for your expensive purchase. There is the good chance that whatever you were told was heavy on misinformation that was at best silly and at worst downright dangerous to the bird.

On the other hand, you may have bought your parrot from a breeder. In this case, the breeder probably gave you a good deal of sound advice about how to care for the bird. You were probably given recommendations for one or two good avian veterinarians and encouraged to get your new parrot a physical examination and routine lab work to ensure that it was healthy at the point of sale and would remain so.

However, you may not have taken all that good information very seriously. Perhaps you only half-listened. After all, how hard can it be to take care of a parrot, right? And you may not have sought a new bird checkup, either. Veterinarians are costly, and you had already spent a young fortune on the bird. Besides, it looked and acted just fine when you got it. Right?

**Feather pickers often resemble
well-used dusters.**

Now your bird picks its feathers. The gorgeous, exotic creature you brought home and so proudly showed off to family and friends now looks a like moth-eaten feather duster that has seen far better days. How much pleasure can you take in something so ugly? It's a downright shame, and you're feeling very angry with the bird. It picked a pretty poor way to repay you for all the care and money you lavished on it.

Or perhaps your bird bites. Hard. Every time you go near it. Now this is really upsetting, because your friend down the street has a Blue-fronted Amazon that simply adores her. It grieves when she's out of its sight, would rather sit on her shoulder than

Or your parrot screams . . .

anywhere else in the world and would happily give up its favorite treats for life rather than even think of biting her. And into the bargain, her Blue-front talks up a storm. There's simply no end to the clever things that parrot says, and often talks so appropriately it makes your hair stand on end. Why, that bird was one of the reasons you decided you had—simply *had*—to have a parrot. And look at the miserable, nasty creature now! It's plain mean, and you just might have to have it put down. The only reason you haven't is that you really hate to see all that money go down the drain. Perhaps selling it to someone else might be a good alternative?

Or maybe your parrot screams. Night and day. Loud enough to wake the dead. The more you tell it to shut up, the louder it screams. Your significant other has begun to issue ultimatums—me or the bird, one of us has to go. Your landlord is making ugly noises about either your getting rid of the bird or his getting rid of you. Living in a tent in your parents' back yard has very little appeal. If only the bird would just shut up! You're getting to the point where you hate the sight of it. Your life is well on the way to becoming a shambles because of the cursed bird. Brother, did you make a mistake on this one! If you'd had any idea a parrot could be like this, you would have cut off your arm rather than buy one. Now you're stuck with it, unless you can unload it on some unsuspecting soul. Or maybe you

Rude parrots often cause serious family disagreements.

could move it to the basement. No one goes down there much unless they must, and at least the bird's shrieks will be muffled and more bearable that way.

One or all of the above is reason enough to train your parrot, or, more properly, teach it the skills that allow it to live happily with its human family and allow you to enjoy the parrot—rather than resenting, ignoring, or abusing it, either knowingly or unknowingly. First, the bird is a significant financial investment. It makes no sense to allow that expenditure to become a waste because you are unable to enjoy the parrot. Second, the presence of an unmanageable pet in your home detracts considerably from the quality of your life and the life of your family. Such a pet is frequently the cause for serious disagreements, arguments, and smoldering resentment on the part of other family members. Obviously, this is not a desirable state of affairs.

Third, and to the author's mind the most important reason for training your parrot, is the bird's quality of life. A parrot is not a dog or cat. It is not a domestic animal, even though it was born in captivity. Thirty-five million years of wild genes do not go away because the egg was hatched in a nestbox or incubator instead of a nesthole in a tree seventy feet above the rainforest floor. However, the parrot is intelligent and adaptable. It is fully capable of learning the few simple behaviors that will enable it to enjoy a happy, healthy life as a cherished member of the family.

Cole

There is no doubting the intelligence of this lovely Blue-fronted Amazon, owned by Mr. and Mrs. Richard Cole.

A parrot's intelligence has been likened to that of a dolphin or whale. This being so, it deserves the blessings and benefits of training and the commitment of the owner that will make this possible. We socialize our children as much for their sakes as for ours. We wish them to become happy, useful members of society, able to function in all the ways adults are expected to function in our world. Most of us would not think of allowing our children to grow up as wild beings, devoid of a notion of what constitutes reasonable behavior. It is no different for a parrot. It is a grave disservice to neglect to teach it good manners and the skills it must have to become the companion its great potential will allow if properly guided.

There is nothing as sad as the wreck of a formerly beautiful, happy parrot because its owners did not understand what a parrot really is, and how to work with it so it could remain the pet they'd expected to have. There is Max, for example. A once lovely Mollucan Cockatoo, he was originally acquired by a businessman who thought it would add a touch of class to his establishment to have a large parrot in the reception room. It was only a matter of weeks before he realized that his bird was more than a decoration. It was loud; it was messy; and it demanded attention. No one was willing to deal with the reality of caring properly for the bird, so it was relegated to the basement of the building for three years, without toys or companionship—the equivalent of human solitary

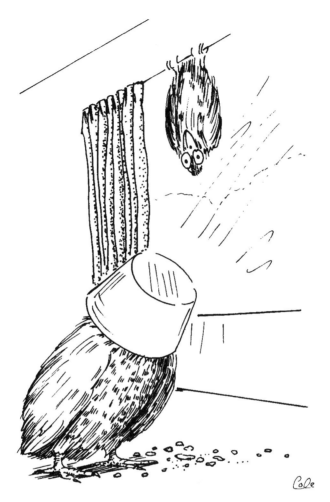

Parrots must be appreciated for what they are.

confinement. To make matters worse, although it hardly seems believable, when everyone went home on Friday at five o'clock to enjoy the weekend, the lights were switched off all over the building, including the basement. Max, therefore, lived every weekend for three years in pitch darkness.

When the cockatoo came to the author's attention, it was receiving treatment for a hole it had chewed in its chest muscle, as well as self-mutilation of its wing webs. It had destroyed every feather it could reach and was nearly bald. Filthy, smelly, and infinitely sad, Max came home with me. His prognosis was very poor. It is a great testimony to the hardihood of the bird's essential spirit that Max remained gentle and sweet in spite of the horror that had been his for the first three years of his life. He has responded to light and air, to the companionship of my other pet birds, and to a good diet and appropriate attention. He has allowed his feathers to regrow, although he still clips off his flight and tail feathers. He no longer mutilates his own flesh. He is happy and healthy. Perhaps one day he'll allow his magnificent wing and tail feathers to grow out. Anything is possible for a bird of Max's great spirit.

The sad thing about Max's case is that his former owner's expectations of him were shallow and of his own devising. They had nothing to do with what the bird really was, nor with the bird's needs. The owner was never able to learn and appreciate what a dear creature Max was. Nor was he interested in working with Max to provide him with a decent quality of life. The outer bird was all that mattered; the inner bird did not interest him. Max will in all likelihood never have completely perfect plumage, but he is himself—and precious for that reason alone.

Parrots must be appreciated for what they are, not for what we want them to be or think they should be. We must not be so eager to throw up our hands in disgust and give up because we are unable or unwilling to acknowledge our own part in creating the "monster." Yes, the parrot must learn for its own well-being what is expected of it in the family setting. But at the same time, we must learn to shed our often inappropriate ideas and conceptions of what a parrot should be. We also need to identify the feelings that may be preventing us from developing a positive relationship with the bird. A parrot with its own agenda—and the author has never met a parrot that didn't have its own agenda—can nevertheless be the most delightful companion on earth.

Max's story can be told with many variations by every serious bird owner and breeder in the country. Fortunately, many of these parrots reach safe harbor when they are placed with knowledgeable and loving owners who possess the commitment, skill, and patience to improve and augment the parrots' life quality. The point, however, is that in many, many cases had the parrot been given the training and socialization required for living in the domestic setting by its first owner, it would never have needed to be removed from its original home. Both the bird and the owner would have been spared much misery.

If you have a parrot with behavior problems, do not despair. With effort, love, and commitment, these unwanted behaviors can be modified or, in some cases, entirely eradicated. You will then have given that parrot a priceless gift—the gift of being able to return to the "flock," an appreciated, loved companion, with all the privileges and supervised freedom inherent in a mutual friendship of the parrot/human type.

Train your parrot. Socialize your parrot. It is the kindest thing you can ever do for it.

What Is a Parrot?

Before we can get on with the subject of "Just how do you train a parrot, anyway?" we need to examine what a parrot really is, and why you wanted one. The answers to these questions can provide a good deal of insight into how you approach working with your bird. The basic techniques will remain the same, but will nearly always require some modification to tailor them to your and your parrot's individual situations. Too, looking honestly at your motivation for having this sometimes frustrating and always fascinating creature in your life will help you determine how to modify your own ideas and feelings about the bird so you can work more effectively with it.

Generally speaking, living and working with a parrot—if it is to be a good experience for both you and the bird—is essentially a Zen experience. There is no place here for rigidity, predetermined expectations, or quick fixes. The process is all. Being with the process, going with the flow, relaxing and enjoying the humor of living with a perpetual three-year-old that nevertheless has the capacity to transform your life, and finding meaning in the moment and the sacred in the profane are really what it's all about. The relationship of parrot and human is in constant flux. What it is today is not what it was yesterday, nor what it will be tomorrow. It is the same as a friendship with another human. Variety and change are at the heart of every relationship. The needs of each participant will change from day to day. One day, one individual's needs will take precedence; another day, it will be the other's needs that must be addressed and cared for. Mutual respect provides the context in which this can take place easily and lovingly, without the unhealthy, unwanted result of one of the pair dominating to the detriment of the other.

This being said, a parrot is then to you—what? Did you expect much less or much more of it when you first purchased it? Be very honest with yourself.

Let's see. A parrot is . . .

A Parrot Is a Bird

Obvious, yes. But, ah—wait! Birds are the only living dinosaurs left in this world. Therefore, your parrot is a dinosaur, the modern version of a proud and ancient race. Look into your parrot's eyes and see the old, old wisdom, the "knowing" that is there. Respect it. It is a wisdom very different from yours, but it exists and demands recognition. This parrot wisdom allows the bird to see things very differently than you do. We must understand that when parrots do things we don't approve of, we're seeing their behavior from the human perspective. What may seem wrong and inappropriate to us often makes very good sense from the parrot's

Parrots are wild animals that have evolved over millions of years. The earliest known parrot-like fossils are 53 million years old!

viewpoint. Case in point: Your parrot is on your arm and your husband walks into the room. Your parrot can't stand your husband, but does he bite your spouse? He does not. He may, however, very well bite you! The reason for this behavior is that the bird sees your spouse as a rival or a creature who threatens you—whom he perceives to be his mate—and he bites you in an effort to drive you away from "danger," or the attentions of a "rival."

Parrots showing persistent behavior problems
should be seen by an avian veterinarian.

This leads us to another characteristic of parrots. *They are wild.* Their instinctive responses are those of a wild creature. These instincts and responses have allowed parrots to survive for millions of years. However, these same responses can and do cause many problems for parrots and their owners in the domestic setting, because we do not understand and often misinterpret them.

A parrot shares many of the same aspects of anatomy and body (physiology) as humans and other mammals, but there are also significant differences. For this reason, any parrot showing behavioral problems or changes should always be seen by a qualified avian veterinarian. Most veterinarians who treat small animals are not knowledgeable about birds and will not be able to provide the care a parrot needs. Birds showing personality changes may well be ill, so never assume such a parrot is just being "ornery," or that the present aberration will "pass." Before embarking on any training program, always first rule out the possibility of illness. Not only is it essential that a sick bird receive care as quickly as possible, but attempting to train such a bird will only stress it further, and may even cause its death.

Parrots Are by Nature Messy

Not dirty, messy. If a parrot is maintained in a constant state of filth, the owner is at fault, not the bird. In the wild, parrots are fastidious. Nesting chambers are kept very clean and tidy by parent birds. Unwanted food is discarded and falls to the ground below, along with droppings. In nature, then, the bird does not live in close proximity to its refuse. It does not create a source of dirt and contamination. In the domestic setting, it does. The parrot has no choice but to defecate where it is, whether it is in its cage, on the floor, or on the furniture. The caged parrot continues to fling unwanted food away, a natural behavior. Hopefully, discarded food sails to the bottom of the cage. More often than not, it lands on the floor to be scattered by a family member or the current from powerful wing beats as the parrot performs its daily "jazzercise." Until one has lived with a parrot, one does not fully realize that the cleanup is never-ending. The realization can come as rather a shock.

Parrots Are Noisy

The really large species, such as cockatoos and macaws, have powerful voices designed to carry over long distances. This allows them to stay in vocal contact with mates, offspring, and other members of the flock. They particularly like to vocalize at daybreak and at dusk. At these times birds are together in the wild. In the morning, being very social creatures, they communicate with other flock members to ascertain who's there and who isn't, who made it through the night, the state of the weather and their surroundings, where to forage for the best fruit,

Cleanups are never-ending.

and other parrot priorities about which we can only guess. At dusk, it's pretty much the same thing—an "It's nine of the clock and all's well," much in the same manner the town crier in colonial times assured the townsfolk that no enemies had been sighted, the river was within its banks, and all worthy citizens could go to their beds with the fair assurance that they'd see the next sunrise.

Parrots, of course, see no difference between living in a tree and living in a house when it comes to these morning and evening vocalizations. Most are apt to be quite noisy during these times and owners must simply resign themselves to this. Problem screaming is something else again. But morning and evening communication from the parrot to its human flock is only to be expected. It's part of living with a parrot.

The parrot grapevine.

Parrots Are Flock Animals

Living in a flock has numerous advantages for the individual as well as the flock as a whole. The individual bird benefits by all the extra eyes and ears available to warn of danger. In the same way, the entire flock will be alerted to danger when the individual sounds the warning call. Information about the best forag-ing areas and water supplies is available to every flock member through the "parrot grapevine." Also, as youngsters are recruited into the breeding popula-tion of the flock, a choice of acceptable mates is readily available. And very importantly, the individual parrot is always surrounded by its own family as well as the "extended family" of the flock as a whole. There is companionship in the flock; the individual never has to feel alone or lonely. This has extremely impor-tant consequences for the owner working with his or her parrot to modify unwanted behavior: Because the parrot will see its human family as its flock, isolation of the bird—"time out" away from its human flock—is a very effective means of discipline.

The fact that parrots are flock animals has another important consequence for their owners: The bird is genetically programmed to seek dominance in the flock, just as wild dogs and wolves do in their packs. It is also programmed to recognize and submit to the dominant member. In the family setting, this means *you*. This is accomplished by gentle but firm guidance, *never* with physical punishment and/or abuse.

The primary caretaker is not always first in the parrot's affections.

Parrots Are Selective

Just the fact that you bought the parrot, provided its cage, toys, and treats, clean up after it, and talk to it does not mean the bird will view you as its best friend. Often, of course, this will be the case. But it is not at all uncommon for the parrot to conceive a passion for the very person who has the least to do with its care. This may be frustrating and maddening, but is all too true. Along these same lines, a parrot will usually not relate to people it does not know. Here again, its wild instincts come into play: Anything new, strange, or unknown spells danger in the wild. A parrot is genetically programmed to avoid such things, and it will do the same in the family setting. Just because your Uncle Josh loves birds and fancies himself the Pied Piper of Parrotdom doesn't mean he won't receive a nasty bite from your avian friend if it thinks he is taking unwarranted liberties. Parrots aren't dogs or cats, genetically predisposed to relate kindly to those of the human persuasion. They never will be.

Parrots Are Long-Lived

The parrot in your life may very well outlive you, especially if you have chosen a large macaw, cockatoo, or Amazon. This means that you both have a lifetime to spend on your mutual friendship. Nothing need be rushed. There will be time enough for everything. Friendship with a parrot is a leisurely, elegant thing. It should have none of the qualities of the frenzied race of modern life with its superficial relationships and fifteen-second sound-byte quality. Friendship with a parrot is iced tea on a lazy, sun-flecked summer afternoon, not a brittle "We must meet for lunch one day soon" over quick drinks at a noisy, impersonal cocktail party.

Friendship with a parrot is a leisurely thing.

Parrots have an offbeat, puckish sense of humor.

Parrots Are Affectionate and Loyal with Those They Know and Love

It still amazes me when I hear a soft cluck and look up from my computer to see my stocky Yellow-naped Amazon round the office door to visit me. My office is on the second floor of our home, at the opposite end of the house from the family room where Ollie lives. Those short little legs have had to travel a distance and climb a long flight of stairs to be with me. It makes me feel humble and very blessed.

Parrots Are Very Intelligent

Many parrots learn meaningful speech. Many possess an off-beat, puckish sense of humor that makes living with them a constant adventure. They are curious and adaptable, and capable of learning the social behaviors they need to live happily with their human families. In general, they are like two- or three-year-olds that never grow up. They must therefore be treated with the same firm, loving discipline one would use with a toddler. They must also be protected from the hazards existing in any household—electric cords, open toilets, hot liquids on the stove, and on and on. Welcome to nurseryland!

Why Did You Want a Parrot?

The reasons we want parrots in our lives have a great deal to do with how successful or unsuccessful our relationships with them are. Because of this, the owner who has a "problem" parrot must be willing to examine his or her reasons for having one before any meaningful change can be made in the situation. Why? Because the parrot does not react in an emotional, social vacuum. When you do or don't do something, the parrot reacts to this. Then you react to the parrot's response. It then reacts to yours, and on and on. It is certainly true that many of the bird's reactions are instinctual, but only up to a point. The great majority of the bird's behavioral repertoire is learned behavior—learned as a result of its experience and interaction with its surroundings and owner.

It is also certainly true that when another individual, either avian or human, fails to fulfill our expectations, we often become angry, resentful, and frustrated—and eventually avoid contact with the cause of our emotional discomfort. It is only human nature to walk away from such situations, because in addition to all the other uncomfortable feelings we can have, we can suspect that somehow we have failed. And no one likes to fail. We especially don't like the feeling of failure at the hands—or claws, if you will—of a mere bird! It's too demeaning and embarrassing. Also, if we fancy ourselves "good with animals," we just might feel secretly that we've been made to appear foolish.

Until we confront our feelings about the relationship with the parrot, we can make no progress toward identifying and healing whatever difficulty may exist. Many problems develop because we wanted the bird for the wrong reasons. Remember Max? So . . . it is necessary to be honest with ourselves, and to decide up front what it is we want from the bird. For example, if you merely want a talented talker to occupy a cage and provide entertainment, perhaps the parrot's aggressive behavior can be tolerated. If, on the other hand, you are disturbed that your parrot's behavior makes it impossible for it ever to leave the cage, you may want to make a commitment to teach the bird acceptable behavior that will enable it more freedom and interaction with its human flock—something sure to improve any parrot's emotional health and quality of life.

The following are all reasons why people acquire parrots. All are poor reasons for owning a parrot.

- They want the amusement value of a talented talking bird.

- A large parrot with a powerful beak, perched upon the owner's shoulder, sends (so the owner hopes) the message that the owner is also powerful and charismatic.

- The owner wishes a touch of the exotic in his or her home or work environment.

- The parrot provides a link, however weak, with a wild world that is disappearing at a horrifying rate, and which most of us will never experience on a more personal, immediate level.

- The parrot provides a vivid, living complement to the decorative scheme of the owner's home.

- The expense and rarity of some parrots (some may cost as much as $15,000) show off the economic status of the owner, who wants to ensure that no one can possibly mistake his or her privileged financial rank in life.

- The owner wants a pet for his or her children, for various reasons, particularly if allergies prevent having a cat or dog in the home.

When the parrot behaves as a living creature with needs and agendas of its own, refusing to fit in quietly and passively with its owner's ideas, trouble is sure to follow. And in nearly every case, the parrot is the loser.

The last item in the above list requires a brief explanation. *Parrots are not good pets for children.* These birds are prone to interpret the boisterous voices and rapid movements of children as a threat and bite in self-defense. Many species, notably the cockatoos, African Greys, and cockatiels, produce powder down that they use to groom their feathers. Children who are allergic to cats and dogs will probably be allergic to this powder down and bird dander. Also, very few adults are willing to spend the time supervising the parrot and the child when they are together. *Children should never be left alone with parrots, even the small parrot species such as budgies and cockatiels.* The chance for harm to both child and bird is too great.

There is only one good reason to own a parrot: because one wants to have a lifelong, loyal, loving pet. The owner should be willing to provide for the parrot's needs for its entire life (or as long as the owner lives) and to give it everything it must have to be healthy, happy, and secure—physically, emotionally, mentally, and spiritually. It is a great responsibility and must never be taken lightly.

Don't despair, though, if your own motives were less than "noble and pure" when you bought your parrot. By now, you have become attached to the little critter and want to make things better—otherwise you wouldn't be reading this book. So read on. With time and a willing heart, great things can be accomplished. If you've decided that maybe your expectations of the parrot and your reasons for buying it could have been unfair to the bird, you've made the first big step. If you've decided that perhaps that wretched creature is behaving the way it is for a pretty good reason and that the behavior is a cry for help, you're even further ahead. If you've decided that a genuine two-way friendship with your parrot is really what you want, even if it did take you a little while to figure it out, then you and your parrot friend are really on your way!

What Has Been Learned in This Chapter?

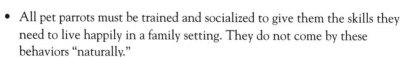

At the end of every chapter (except chapter 5) is a quick review of the major points covered. This serves as a refresher to help you better remember the most important points intraining and teaching these birds, whether you're starting fresh with a newly acquired parrot or healing a relationship with the parrot you already have.

- All pet parrots must be trained and socialized to give them the skills they need to live happily in a family setting. They do not come by these behaviors "naturally."

- Parrots that have been properly trained and socialized will enjoy a much better level of social, emotional, mental, and spiritual well-being than those that have not received such training.

- All parrots should be checked regularly by a qualified avian veterinarian to ensure their continued good health. A bird whose behavior has changed suddenly and radically is probably ill.

- Sick birds should not be involved with training because of the increased stress and its effects on the bird's already poor health. The bird must be restored to good health before training of any kind can take place.

- Parrots are ancient and, as with all birds, are the modern versions of dinosaurs.

- Parrots are intelligent, long-lived, and adaptable.

- Parrots are flock animals in the same way dogs and wolves are pack animals. Because of this, the pet parrot in the home enjoys and needs the company of its human companions.

- Because parrots are flock animals, they have a drive for dominance in the flock and will also exercise this drive in the family setting. For this reason, the owner must establish his or her dominance as the "alpha" bird by use of consistent firm yet gentle guidance.

- Parrots can be very affectionate and loyal to their chosen humans.

- A parrot will not necessarily choose you as its favorite human simply because you are the primary caregiver.

- Parrots should not be expected to be friendly to those with whom they are not familiar.

- Some parrot behavior is instinctive and cannot be changed. The owner must be willing to allow the bird a reasonable amount of "parrotness."

- The only acceptable reason for wanting or owning a parrot is to enjoy a lifelong, mutually rewarding friendship with one of the most fascinating creatures on earth.

P.S. A parrot's friendship and trust are its greatest gifts and not conferred just because the owner could afford the purchase price of the bird.

2

Normal Parrot Behavior

Knowledge is no burden.

—English proverb

Very often many of the difficulties we encounter with our parrots stem from our lack of understanding of normal parrot behavior. For those readers who aren't going through rough patches with their parrots, please read this chapter anyway. Forewarned is forearmed, and potential difficulties can thus be avoided. For those experiencing problems with their birds, this chapter gives the basis for a more satisfying mutual relationship with a pet parrot. Without this knowledge, the training techniques in the following chapters will not be nearly as effective.

There must be an emotional connection between both of you in order for the relationship you seek to begin working. Understanding is the beginning of acceptance and affection. If this happens, at some time—and this time cannot be predicted, because each parrot/human relationship is unique—some rather miraculous things will begin to happen. They are intangible, and it is impossible to tell exactly how they occur, but they do. They are precious and are the rewards of those willing to invest in forming a sincere, genuine emotional bond with their parrots.

As was noted in chapter 1, many parrot behaviors are instinctive, and although they can be modified to a certain extent, they cannot be completely

We often do not know how to care for our parrots properly.

changed or eradicated. As with so many other things in life, "All things in moderation" applies to your bird's behavior. Most parrot owners are able to live happily with these traits provided they know such behaviors are normal and predictable. When ordinary, expected behavior spirals out of control, or when we, for some reason, are not able to accept these normal behaviors at the moderate levels all healthy, happy, well-adjusted parrots display, problems almost always occur.

Understanding the latter is very important to avoid creating "problem parrots." If concerned owners learn how to forge mutually rewarding friendships with their parrots, ignorance will no longer provide the fertile field for the development of misunderstanding and the strife it will cause.

However, we don't always try to learn what makes our feathered companions tick, even if we know we can't accept the knowledge or put it to use. In the absence of our understanding, genuine, chronic, hard-to-correct problems begin and, if not remedied quickly, will snowball. But if we truly desire to improve a bad situation, we must now, however painfully and reluctantly, accept our own part in the creation of any problems. With very rare exceptions, we foster our birds' problems in the following ways:

- We do not know how to care for and handle parrots properly.

- We know what to do, but choose not to act on our awareness.

- We have acted as enablers of our parrots' undesirable behavior for reasons that have more to do with our own needs than those of our birds.

Problems do not occur in a vacuum. It is true that parrots are not hatched with a natural affinity for humans. But they are born with a very strong drive to bond with and be a member of a social group, and to confer a particular affection on a mate—which, in the wild, will be a lifelong companion. These instincts prepare parrots to accept people and to live with human love and companionship.

Defining Normal Parrot Behavior

What, then, can we expect to label "normal" parrot behavior? "Normal" is, of course, a relative term. It is normal for any animal that feels mortally threatened to flee or otherwise defend itself. It is normal for a nesting hen parrot to bite when her nestbox is invaded. It is not normal for an unprovoked animal to bite. However, what passes for unprovoked to us may indeed appear entirely different to the animal in question. If the animal happens to be a mature Amazon, especially one that has not been well reared, it may attack its owner in response to

Free to a good home!

**Owners of large parrots are pretty used to noise
that might upset owners of smaller birds!**

what the owner describes as a nonthreatening behavior. But if the parrot is staking out its breeding territory, it will defend it against all comers. What provokes an attack depends upon viewpoint, and the parrot's is often totally different from the owner's.

In spite of all this, there are certain behaviors we can identify as normal. We can expect them in family settings, and they need not be viewed as deviant unless they escalate to the point that the entire family is threatening to put us and our birds out on the curb with a sign that says "Free to a good home!"

We must also be aware that each of us has a different tolerance level for various kinds of parrot behavior. If you are the owner of a large macaw or cockatoo, you are probably pretty blasé about the morning and/or evening blasts that assault your ears on a daily basis. On the other hand, the owner of a cockatiel or budgie would probably find them absolutely intolerable.

Further, we must accept that some perfectly standard behaviors in one species are, in some cases, almost unknown in others. For example, Amazon parrots are generally very noisy and delight in screeching and vocalizing. Most African

All parrots preen a lot.

parrots (African Greys, Meyer's Parrots, Senegals, Jardine's Parrots, etc.), on the other hand, tend to be much quieter. Greys, especially, once they learn to speak, rarely scream unless badly frightened. They much prefer to talk, whistle, and make a particularly musical "hooting" sound.

All of the above means that even though we can speak in generalities about "normal and expected" behavior, much is dependent on the species, the individual of that species, and the owner's tolerance. Every case is individual, and each parrot/human pair must determine what constitutes the acceptable—within educated reason. This is part of the bottom line. The other part is that we must be willing to allow the parrot to be a parrot. We cannot transform it into a dog, ever willing to do our slightest bidding; a quiet, aloof house cat; a canary, or anything else. Your friend *is* a parrot, and will *remain* a parrot; that never changes. The difference between enjoying a wonderful friendship with pet birds and devising imaginary tortures of a terrible and exotic nature for the *feathered fiend* making our lives miserable rests almost solely on us, our birds' protectors and guardians. As we direct, the relationship develops.

Preening and Molting (or, Maintaining a Decent Wardrobe Is Pure Hell!)

All birds preen as if the love of their lives will suddenly appear and be awestruck by the glorious plumage and winsomely seductive manner of this mate of its dreams.

Preening is the bird's way of distributing the oil or powder down with which it dresses its feathers, rendering them waterproof and keeping them clean. Preening also "knits" together the separated feather barbs so that the feather will have maximum efficiency in flight. When parrots preen, down feathers will be loosened and lost, as will the occasional body (contour) feather. This is normal and not a cause for concern. During a major molt, large tail and flight feathers will also drop. Nor do we need to worry about what sometimes seems an unusually high proportion of time spent preening. This is perfectly normal behavior and necessary to the health of the bird's plumage.

All birds molt (discard) old feathers on a regular basis. When this occurs depends on the amount of daylight, the temperature, and the parrot's breeding condition, health, and nutritional level. Parrots living indoors with artificial heat may molt a few feathers all year long. Many, however, tend to molt after what would be the normal breeding season in the wild. I have noticed that in my own breeding birds, the parents tend to molt heavily after the babies have left the nest. By the time new feathers have grown in, they are ready to enjoy the "off-season" and are in shining plumage when they once again go through the cycle of courtship and chick rearing.

During a heavy molt, several flight and tail feathers will be lost, in addition to numerous body feathers. Nature has arranged for most birds (parrots included) to always have enough feathers to become airborne should danger threaten.

As feathers are lost, new feathers begin to grow in. They are encased in a sheath of keratin, which looks a great deal like a thin layer of fingernail material. New feathers can be very scratchy and uncomfortable while they are growing in, and your parrot will spend much time preening the new feathers in order to remove the sheath and allow the feather to unfurl. *During this time, it may seem cranky and nippy.* This is because these "blood feathers" are tender, and scratching or petting your parrot too vigorously at this time can cause it pain. You don't need to stop handling the bird during a molt; just be gentler than usual when petting and playing with it. And take your cue from the parrot's behavior. If it seems uncomfortable, return it to the perch or cage for a time. Don't force your attentions. Your parrot will appreciate your consideration.

When bald patches appear, you should be concerned about preening or molting. When you see your parrot deliberately pull out feathers, this is very different from the molting feather that falls out effortlessly as the parrot preens. Feathers not ready to molt must be forcibly plucked out, and you will be able to see this easily—the parrot really has to work at it. Concern is also in order if the bird deliberately breaks off, or "clips" a feather. Molts that go on and on, without regeneration of healthy new plumage, are a cause for concern. So are new feathers that have grown in misshapen, discolored, or fragile. If you bird shows any of these symptoms, take it to a qualified avian veterinarian. Underlying health problems usually exist in these cases and require treatment. See *The Parrot in Health and Illness* (New York: Howell Book House, 1991), by this author, for an in-depth discussion of feather-related problems.

If you share your life and home with a parrot, expect to vacuum the area around the cage on a daily basis to get rid of the little down feathers and feather dust that will constantly accumulate.

Eating Habits (or, Occupational Therapy for the Housebound Parrot!)

Parrots are quite dainty eaters and great fun to watch when they're "at table," as the nineteenth-century English were wont to say. I love to see one of my birds holding a favorite morsel with his foot, chewing appreciatively, eyes cast heavenward with what appears to be an expression of pure bliss. Parrots are also very careful to clean their beaks after eating, by scrupulously wiping them on the perch. (A very good reason to keep perches spotlessly clean!) They then finish off the toilette with a vigorous cleaning of the beak with a foot. If you're really in luck, your parrot may swipe its beak on your starched, white business shirt or that new Liz Claiborne blouse you paid a fortune for and are wearing for the first time.

Parrots are quite dainty eaters.

Into the laundry with this blouse!

What is definitely *not* dainty about your parrot's eating habits is its normal tendency to toss about discarded food! Parrots have an excellent sense of taste. They also have no sense of "waste not, want not." Favored tidbits will be attacked enthusiastically, but when friend parrot has eaten enough, the remainder will be tossed disdainfully to the cage bottom or onto your nice, clean floor. Often, while rummaging in the food bowl for that just-right piece of carrot or corn on the cob, a parrot will gleefully shovel the rest of the contents out, scattering them far and wide. And if boredom sets in, it may pepper the surrounding area with uneaten pellets just for the sheer entertainment value.

All this is perfectly normal behavior. In the wild, parrots have no need for cleaning devices of any kind. They simply throw unwanted "stuff" off the branch, and that's that. Of course, they have no need for cleaning tools in the domestic setting, either. That's why they had the wit to retain a housemaid—guess who? Parrots are perfectly happy to let you do the never-ending cleanup in exchange for the encouragement of their company.

If you share your life and home with a parrot, plan to vacuum the area around the cage on a daily basis. Sound familiar? Also, keep a spray bottle of half white vinegar and half water handy. It's simply murder to clean up yesterday's veggie mash à la Savarin without it.

Parrots delight in throwing discarded food as far as they can.

Doane

Mac, the author's beloved Timneh African Grey,
samples washed grapes at the kitchen sink.

Chewing (or, A Bird's Gotta Do What a Bird's Gotta Do!)

Parrots love to chew—anything and everything. There is no discrimination between the ten dollar chew toy you just bought your bird and your very expensive Mies van der Rohe chair. We used to think that parrots chewed to keep their beaks trim, and perhaps they do. But the fact is, their beaks stay trim with or without chewing material. A bird with an overgrown beak has a serious health problem, the most likely being a severely fatty liver—a condition that needs immediate attention by your avian veterinarian.

A parrot is just as happy chewing an expensive chair as its own toys.

Please don't misunderstand—parrots must have appropriate chewing material. It serves a very necessary psychological purpose. But no matter how many wonderful chewies you've provided, don't expect your parrot to refrain from chewing your furniture, cabinets, or anything else it can get its beak into. Parrots don't think to themselves, "I'm going to leave this gorgeous sofa alone because Dad just got me that spiffy thirty-dollar chew toy. I'll just go back to my cage and chew on that." It will never happen.

The moral of this story is to provide plenty of appropriate chewing material, and *never* let your parrot out of its cage unsupervised. If you do, you will have no one to blame but yourself if your bird does considerable damage to your possessions. Further, the parrot is just as apt to chew on an electrical wire as a dining room chair. The consequences of that don't even bear considering!

Independence of Heart (or, I'm Royalty. Who Are You?)

In many ways, parrots are like cats. They can be aloof, proud, and exceedingly independent. A parrot will never, ever do anything merely to please a human, especially one with whom it hasn't bonded. Whatever a person wants a parrot to do, it must be something to which the parrot agrees, for whatever parrotly reason, before it acquiesces. Humility and subservience are not parrot traits! Understand, please, that once a parrot has given you its trust and affection, it can do amazing things you'd never guess.

I'm reminded of Piper, a Blue-fronted Amazon belonging to Gayle Soucek, current president of the Midwest Avian Research Expo. Piper frequently models for Gayle's business. Working on deadline, Gayle arrived home unexpectedly late one night. The photos had to be taken, and there was nothing to do but wake Piper up and take the shots. Yawning, Piper went through his rather complicated paces with the good-natured grace of a famous and sought-after movie star at a boring but necessary publicity "do." He wouldn't do this for just anyone. But for Gayle—well, that's another matter altogether!

Generally speaking, however, parrots prefer to retreat from any kind of threat, unpleasantness, or unwanted activity. This leads us to one of the most common causes of difficulties between bird and human: the failure to trim the bird's wing feathers and keep them trimmed. Doing so is critical in the first stages of bonding and training. Further, it prevents the parrot from flying into mirrors, out of open doors, into open toilets, into pots of hot liquid on the stove, and from encountering any other hazards of the average household. It is not within the scope of this book to go into detail about wing feather trimming. If the reader is interested in pursuing the subject, such a discussion can be found in *My Parrot, My Friend: An Owner's Guide to Parrot Behavior* (New York: Howell Book House, 1994), by this author. I only wish to state here that to refrain from trimming your parrot's wing feathers will not only fail to provide it with a "natural life," it will expose it to many household dangers and seriously retard your ability to bond with your parrot, and it with you.

Take your parrot to an avian vet or someone else very experienced in performing wing feather trims. Have the person show you how to do it. Although the procedure is simple once you know how—it is no different than clipping your own fingernails and causes the parrot no discomfort at all—you should not attempt it until you are absolutely sure you know what you're doing and can identify growing feathers (blood feathers) with ease and accuracy. Otherwise, the risk of hemorrhage from such a feather is great and requires that the damaged blood feather be pulled out to stop the bleeding. *Never* attempt to trim a parrot's wing feathers without another person assisting you. You will need your assistant to restrain the parrot, leaving your hands free to do the trimming.

The importance of wing feather trimming to the parrot's safety is obvious. What is not so evident to most people is the psychological aspects involved in wing trimming. As previously noted, parrots much prefer to avoid what they perceive as unpleasant or undesirable situations. If the bird is able to fly, it will do just that. This is especially unfortunate in the early stages of your relationship with the bird, when you should be getting to know each other. The parrot must

**Dive-bombing family members is an effective way for
the flighted parrot to protect its territory.**

learn that being in your company is pleasant, not something to be avoided. If your parrot knows it is free to leave whenever it wishes, it may never learn this simple fact. Under such circumstances, bonding is delayed and may never be completely achieved.

This is a real problem with newly weaned, domestically reared youngsters, as well as with newly acquired adult parrots. It is foolish to think that just because a parrot is very young, it will not have or exercise its drive for independence. The youngster must begin to do this as soon as it leaves the protection of its parents' nest, because it then must make its own way in the flock. Weaklings and the timid do not survive very long in the wild. This, then, makes it very important to begin the young parrot's socialization into a human group as soon as it arrives in your home.

The second problem, and a very serious one, occurs with birds who have been allowed free flight and who have reached sexual maturity. Instinctively, these parrots begin to stake out their territory. If they have the run of the house, the entire house becomes this territory. They will then defend it against all comers, dive-bombing members of the family, biting, and indulging in generally obnoxious behavior. The bird is merely doing what comes naturally. However, this cannot be allowed in the family setting. These serious problems need never occur if free access to all areas of the home is precluded by lack of flight.

I am sure there are those readers who feel that clipping a parrot's wing feathers keeps it from leading a "natural" life. Please understand this: It is impossible for the pet parrot to experience a natural existence as a member of a human household. Leaving it free-flighted will not change this in any way. It will only encourage aggression and failure to bond with its owners and increase its chances of serious injury in an environment for which evolution has not prepared it with built-in warning signals of danger. Further, the bird will be free to leave its droppings wherever it pleases and to destroy your possessions with impunity.

Additionally, parrots able to fly perceive themselves as more dominant than their human companions. This in itself, regardless of the parrot's age, leads to aggression. This will be discussed at greater length in the following section. Please note, however, that owners who have made the mistake of allowing their birds unclipped wing feathers are amazed at the change in their parrots' behavior when they finally have those feathers trimmed. Under these circumstances, formerly aggressive birds very often become docile and sociable, soliciting their humans' attention and thoroughly enjoying it.

Drive for Dominance (or, If You Want to Play, You Gotta Pay!)

All parrots have an instinctive drive for dominance. They want to be number one in any setting, whether in their wild flock or in their human family. In this respect, they are just like wild dogs, wolves, and some of the great apes. There is a very good reason for the dominance drive. The individual attaining the coveted "alpha" spot in its group has first choice of mates, nesting areas, food, and other necessities for its survival in the wild, as well as the all-important task of influencing the gene pool of the next generation.

Obviously, achieving primacy in order to fulfill these needs is not important to the parrot living with a human family. However, the parrot does not realize this. It will continue to strive for this position regardless of the fact that its flock is human and its needs for shelter, food, water, and companionship are automatically met by conscientious owners. How does the parrot act when trying to become the head honcho in its family? Primarily, it will always seek the highest place to perch; and it may bite to assert this position unless properly socialized.

**There is a good reason parrots should never be allowed
to perch higher than their owners' heads.**

The above forms the basis for the rationale of never allowing the parrot to be higher than its humans. When perched on a shoulder or playing on a cage-top gym, the bird actually feels itself to be physically bigger than its humans and will often attempt to enforce its "king of the hill" position by lunging and/or biting. It very often refuses to come up onto the proffered hand or arm from such a position. Or it may lead its owner in a merry game of "catch me if you can," all over the top and sides of the cage. *Much aggressive behavior can be corrected by merely never allowing the bird to be higher than the owner's mid-chest. Parrots should never be allowed higher than this when out of the cage.* To permit this is to invite disaster, if not sooner, then almost certainly later.

The Need to Be Part of a Group

Along with the drive for dominance, parrots have an instinctive need to be part of the group, whether the wild flock or a human family. At first, this may seem contradictory, but note that achieving the alpha position in a wild flock does not prevent the bird from enjoying the advantages of living in a social group. The most important advantage is protection from predators. A flock has a hundred pairs of eyes and ears with which to see and hear danger and give the alarm. In addition, the flock provides companionship, something all parrots crave. The flock furnishes shields against loneliness and isolation. It also provides a pool of potential mates to the individual ready to take its place in the breeding population.

The social group, then, is extremely important to the parrot's mental and spiritual well-being. If it is a member of a human family, it will relate to family members (or a chosen individual within the family) because it needs and craves security and protection. As we mentioned in the first chapter, this becomes a potent tool for nonaggressive, effective parrot discipline. Although the parrot does not understand physical aggression and will always react very negatively to it, it does understand the meaning of isolation. Thus, isolating the bird in an unused room or placing it in its cage and ignoring it for a specified length of time is a very effective means of helping it understand unwanted behavior will not be tolerated. This is very similar to the "time out" technique used with young children. The meaning of discipline will be discussed in more detail later in this chapter.

Pair Bonding (or, 'Til Death Do Us Part!)

Parrots also have the drive to bond, which is sometimes exclusively directed to one human. This is because in the wild, the majority of parrot species are monogamous. They choose a mate and stay with that mate for as long as one or both of them live. There is a good reason for this. Parrots are very long-lived, and in the course of their lives as one of a pair they rear relatively few offspring. This is unlike many song birds, which may raise two or three clutches of four to six youngsters every breeding season. Their chicks are only in the nest for a matter of four weeks or so before fledging. Parrot chicks, however, have very long nestling periods and fledge only when several months old—especially those of the larger species, such as macaws and cockatoos. Even chicks of medium-sized parrots, such as African Greys and Amazons, will be in the nest for three months or so. Caring for the chicks is a huge investment of time and energy resources for the parents. One parent alone would not be able to do the job. It must have the constant help of its mate in order to rear chicks successfully.

To this end, the bond between most parent birds is very strong and is lifelong. The obvious and awesome affection between bonded parrots serves the purpose of keeping the pair together, just as it does in human pairs. The parrot is prepared to bestow this same affection and loyalty on its human owner. Although it may treat all members of the household with tolerance and good-natured regard, it is unusual for a parrot to bond strongly with more than one member of its human family.

There are some parrot species that do not pair bond: *Rosellas*, Ringnecked parakeets, *Eclectus* parrots, and the Australian grass parakeets. They are not as commonly kept as pets, although they are delightful in their own way. Nor do they, in general, require as much emotional attention from their owners. For those readers who are interested in these birds, a fuller discussion can be found in *My Parrot, My Friend*.

Biting (A Girl's Gotta Do What a Girl's Gotta Do!)

All parrots can bite! In fact, most parrots, at one time or another in their lives, *will* bite. It makes no difference whether they were wild-caught and imported (increasingly rare since the enactment of the Wild Bird Conservation Act of 1992, prohibiting the import of wild parrots into the United States) or domestically bred.

Why do parrots bite, especially if they love us? There are several reasons.

First, the parrot may not feel well. I'm reminded of Ollie, my Yellow-naped Amazon. Ollie came to me as a bird who had suffered rather extreme emotional deprivation during his first ten years of life. In addition, his owners had always allowed him free flight. As a result, he was very aggressive and totally unable to be handled. Ollie never has had any tolerance whatsoever for anyone else in our family. But after a couple of weeks, he decided I was an okay person and began to come up on my hand, behaving with amazing docility and affection. Then one night, he decided he didn't want to go into his cage at bedtime. He bit me—very hard. He was testing to see what he could get away with. Bleeding copiously from a nasty puncture at the base of my finger, I told him I wouldn't tolerate that behavior and commanded him to get up on my dripping hand. And he did. He never bit me again—until four years later. I was removing his food bowl after supper, when he simply leaned over and nailed me.

I was shocked. This simply wasn't my Ollie. Unusual behavior in a parrot is sometimes the first and only signal a bird is unwell. Sure enough, the next morning, Ollie refused his breakfast. Two hours later, he was at the veterinarian's office diagnosed with a gut infection that required antibiotic injections twice daily for twenty days. Now Ollie can be a very stubborn grudge holder, and I wondered if his treatments would shatter our relationship. But Ollie never held it against me. He bit me only because he was sick.

Birds will also bite out of fear and defense. A parrot that feels threatened, no matter how tame, will often bite. Strange people or surroundings may trigger such a bite. Alcohol may alter the owner's voice, manner, and actions, creating a

Don't let your parrot perch higher than your shoulder.

sense of "wrongness" and unfamiliarity in the parrot. Unaccustomed noises, a curtain flapping in a breeze, or perhaps even a new toy or food bowl may provoke a bite. Remember, birds instinctively react to unfamiliar things to protect themselves. In the wild, they can fly away. In our homes, they do not have this option, so they may bite. It's the classic flight-or-fight response. It is important to understand that the parrot is not acting out of malice, but toward what it sees as a genuine threat.

Excessive handling by the owner may cause a parrot to bite. The bird's tolerance for handling may be exceeded, especially during molting. Rough petting and play that the parrot interprets as aggression may also initiate a bite. Obviously any kind of teasing will provoke a parrot, and should never be indulged in. Be alert to the signals your parrot gives you. If it becomes restless, or its eyes begin to contract and dilate rapidly, place it gently in its cage for some time to itself. It is much better to avoid a bite, which is a bad experience for the owner as well as the bird. Later in the chapter, I'll discuss parrot threat posture and how to avoid its consequences.

Displacement of anger is another reason parrots bite. If a parrot is frightened or displeased by something or someone, and you happen to be holding it, it may bite you because the object of its fear and anger is unavailable. This may happen at times when the parrot views your spouse or another family member as a rival for your attention, as noted in chapter 1. In addition, the bird may bite you in some situations to drive you, its cherished "mate," away from something it feels threatening and dangerous. Parrots doing this to a parrot mate or companion will only grab a mouthful of feathers. Alas, when they do it to their unfeathered human companions, bruising or actual breaking of skin often occurs.

This is yet another reason not to allow a parrot to perch on shoulders, or in positions above their owners. It is easier to control the bird at chest level, or lower. Further, although it is bad enough to be bitten on the hand or arm, a severe bite on the face is something every owner should carefully avoid—and it can be avoided simply by using a little common sense.

Newly weaned youngsters may gnaw or chew on fingers.

Newly weaned youngsters may gnaw or chew on fingers, which they associate with hand-feeding. They may pump them vigorously in a futile attempt to get formula. Young parrots also explore their surroundings with their mouths, just as young children do. Such a youngster does not discriminate between a toy, a piece of food, or your hand. Although "cute," this behavior should not be encouraged or tolerated. Issue a sharp "No!" and distract the bird with a toy. A parrot that grows up thinking hands are toys will eventually be strong enough to deliver a painful bite. With common sense and commitment to proper socialization of the parrot on the owner's part, dominance biting need never become a problem.

Biting at sexual maturity, when a parrot is protecting its territory, can be troublesome. Many owners experience this behavior when they try removing their parrots from their cages. Again, with proper socialization, this need never become an issue. This is not to say it won't happen occasionally, but it should be the exception for the parrot in breeding condition, not the rule.

Last, sometimes your feathered friend simply gets up on the wrong side of the perch. We all have days when we wake up feeling crabby and things just seem to go steadily downhill for the rest of the day. It's no different for your parrot. Be prepared to give it some space and time to "work things out" during these times.

A cranky parrot is capable of giving a good sharp nip. Let it alone for a bit. Chances are, it will feel more in humor with the world and ready to be its usual sweet self after some time by itself. If not, of course, the veterinarian should be consulted.

Parrot Threat Behavior

We all need to be sensitive to the body language of our parrots. When we pay attention, we find that they often give us very clear indications of their feelings. When they bow their heads and ruffle their neck feathers, we know they want a comfortable scratch. When their eyes droop, we know they're sleepy. When we talk to them and they turn their backs, it's a pretty good indication they're seriously displeased with us and are sulking.

**A parrot's body posture usually gives a pretty
good indication of what it is feeling.**

Parrots also let us know when they mean business. Everyone who lives with a parrot should become familiar with these threat postures and what they mean. By doing so, we can avoid a great deal of unpleasantness.

Most times, our parrots let us know when we need to back off. When we ignore these signals, we really deserve the painful nip we probably get. Parrots in the wild signal their potential aggressiveness with body language. In this situation, the other bird will back off and a confrontation will be avoided. Discretion is always the better part of valor in parrot-to-parrot social interaction. We need to do the same thing. This is not "giving in" to the parrot or "letting it have its own way." The

Most parrots let us know when we should back off.

parrot is interacting in a way it perceives as natural and instinctive, and by which it seeks to avoid rather than engage in violent confrontation. Naturally, the parrot that rules the roost with this behavior has a problem, and so does the owner who has allowed this situation to develop. This behavior will be discussed at greater length in later chapters. But we do well to heed the parrot that occasionally, not habitually, displays threat postures and warning signals.

When disturbed or threatened, parrots dilate and constrict their pupils in what is known as "pinning." It can be observed in all parrots except those with very dark eyes, such as white cockatoos. It is especially noticeable

Parrots dilate and constrict their pupils rapidly when upset or excited.

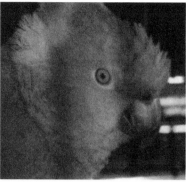

Cole

Cole

A Yellow-naped Amazon with
normally opened pupils.

The same Yellow-naped Amazon
with pupils pinned and contracted.

This parrot has its wings outspread, tail fanned,
and beak open. Watch out!

Beak gaping and eyes pinned is a
common threat posture.

This parrot is signaling its desire
to push an offender away: body
upright, feathers slicked down,
foot raised.

Excited or upset parrots may sway
back and forth on the perch, often
hissing at the same time.

and dramatic in the Amazon species. Pinning may or may not be accompanied by
other threatening body postures.

Examples of parrot threat posture include:

- Crouching low on the perch with wings outspread and tail feathers
  fanned, beak open.

- Wings raised with feathers fanned, beak open.

- Body upright with feathers slicked down and one foot raised to repel the offending person or object.

- Body upright, wings spread, beak open, every feather fluffed out, crest raised (in crested species).

- Swaying back and forth on perch or shifting sinuously from one foot to the other, often accompanied by hissing.

Please note that with cockatoos (and some other parrots), the last two items may indicate pleasurable excitement. The individual situation allows the owner to correctly interpret the subject. *However*, even in these cases, it is wise to let

Soucek

**Is this Moluccan Cockatoo exhibiting threat
or excitement posture? Your job as
owner is to correctly interpret your
parrot's body language.**

your parrot wind down. These birds sometimes seem to "blank out" when really excited and may nip just to nip.

In the other body posture of which we need to be aware, the parrot turns on its back, feet up in the air, belly totally exposed to the threat. It is this posture that parrots display when they have given up all hope of escaping with their lives and lie waiting for death. If your parrot should ever exhibit such behavior, speak calmly and comfortingly to it and have the mercy to walk away and leave it to recover itself. This is a mortally frightening experience for the bird, and it should be shown every kindness and consideration at such times. After the parrot has returned to its perch and seems calm, it can be taken out of its cage to be cuddled and further reassured. But wait until the bird shows you it can tolerate this.

"Last-ditch" posture in a parrot that has surrendered and awaits the inevitable.

What Has Been Learned in This Chapter?

- Parrots possess some traits that are instinctive and could create problems only when they escalate past the normal point for the species.

- An owner's inability to understand and tolerate normal parrot behavior creates problems.

- At times, we must honestly admit to ourselves that our own attitudes and expectations regarding our parrots are unrealistic and need overhauling.

- All parrots preen a great deal.

- All parrots molt worn-out feathers, some heavily during one season; others, irregularly throughout the year.

- Parrots are fastidious in their personal hygiene, but because of their eating, elimination, and daily loss of down feathers, cause messes, with which the owner must be willing to deal.

- All parrots have a chewing instinct and must be supplied with appropriate chewing materials for their psychological health.

- All parrots are extremely independent and do not relate subserviently to their humans, but as "different from but equal to."

- Parrots should never be allowed full flight in the home for reasons of safety and in order to facilitate and maintain the bond with the owner.

- Fully flighted parrots develop problems with territoriality and aggression.

- It is not possible to re-create a "rainforest" life for the parrot living as a companion animal with a family.

- All parrots have an inbred drive for dominance, which will lead to behavior problems if its humans do not socialize and train it properly.

- Parrots should never be allowed to perch higher than the chest level of the person with them outside the cage.

- Parrots are social beings and need to be an active part of the family group.

- Parrots will usually bond strongly with only one family member, although they may relate well to others in the household group.

- All parrots—even hand-reared birds—will occasionally bite, for various reasons, at some time in their lives.

- All owners need to recognize parrot body language and learn what it means.

3

Owner Behavior and Parrot Training

Ignorance is a voluntary misfortune.

—English proverb

To effectively train our parrots, we must also train ourselves. As in any relationship, it takes two. Often we find that some of our own attitudes and behaviors must be changed before we can help our parrots learn and change.

Lack of understanding about what a parrot is and what can and cannot realistically be expected of it is one of the greatest obstacles to helping our birds become active, welcome members of a human family. The previous chapter should have dispelled some inappropriate ideas and shed light on both the capabilities and limitations of your parrot.

We must also be armed with sound information about what discipline really is, along with its absolute necessity. All too often, we equate discipline with punishment; nothing could be farther from the truth. Regarding consistency, we may often take the easy way out—the path of least resistance—but this acts against effective training. There are so many perfectly valid reasons for being lax. We may be tired or not feel well. We may have many pressures and anxieties weighing on us. We may have a family clamoring for our attention, a meal to prepare, a child to chauffeur, an elderly parent requiring care—many things can interfere with our good intentions to set aside quality time to work with our parrots or enforce discipline consistently. It is so natural to think "letting it go one time can't hurt" when our parrots engage in unwanted behavior. But that one time *does* hurt. Nothing is as effective in teaching any animal misbehavior than disciplining one time and letting the next three or four times go unheeded. Psychologists call this intermittent reinforcement, and its use is the death knell for achieving lasting progress in training.

Commitment to providing proper husbandry and nutrition is essential if we expect our parrots to respond positively to our training efforts. A parrot in marginal health, lacking enough sleep, nutritionally compromised, or improperly caged, with all that implies for its emotional health, cannot be expected to respond well to training. Good care and a reasonable routine are necessary for the psychological health of our parrots, and without these elements, progress will be retarded or entirely lacking.

Enabling Unwanted Behavior in Our Parrots

Sometimes, despite what we consider our best efforts to work constructively with our parrots, we just don't seem to get the expected results. At this point, we must look carefully at our own behavior as it relates to our birds. Are we enabling them to misbehave?

At first this may seem a harsh, unreasonable question, especially if our efforts to achieve results seem both futile and frustrating. Enabling unwanted behavior in our animals, or members of our families for that matter, is a subtle but powerful thing, because it operates at a subconscious level and we're never aware of it unless we examine ourselves honestly. Admitting our enabling behavior can be somewhat painful and embarrassing, because it comes squarely from us. It has nothing to do with our parrots at all. It's difficult and humbling to admit to ourselves that *we*, not the bird, may be the real problem. This chapter considers some of the things that may be prompting us subconsciously to enable our parrots to misbehave, or to fail to respond to our training efforts. Once we root them out, we can learn how to prevent them from sabotaging our training efforts.

Centrally related to the issue of enabling is the question of "Why do I want this? Is it for my parrot, or is it my needs alone?" For example, let's look again at the person who wants his or her bird fully flighted. Knowing how dangerous this can be for the bird, and that it is quite impossible to re-create a wild setting in our homes for our birds, do we really want our parrots to fly free? Further, realizing that parrots are rather sedentary creatures that are just as happy to exercise by climbing, flapping their wings, and playing with their toys and human companions, enabling a pet parrot to free flight seems even more unwise. Do we want to see our birds fly freely because we think it's "good" for them, or because it does something for us to see them swooping about? Does some part of us feel restricted and hemmed in? Are we, in fact, symbolically flying free ourselves through the actions of our parrot? Or do we perhaps take a sly and rather secret delight when the parrot harasses another family member with whom we might be at odds? Whose need prompts the owner to allow the bird the danger inherent in free flight, as well as the risk of aggression directed at family members? Is it the owner's or the bird's?

When we enable our birds to misbehave, we are doing so because we get something out of it. Perhaps we feel a sense of pleasurable martyrdom at recounting our troubles with our parrots and the attention this garners from others. Perhaps the parrot's misbehavior serves as a distraction so that we don't have to deal with other serious issues in our lives. Or we may be using the parrot's behavior to punish another family member for some reason. In these cases, triangling and scapegoating may be operating. These concepts are explored in depth in My Parrot, My Friend, for readers who wish to pursue the subject. Another thing to consider honestly is that it may be very important to us that the parrot relate exclusively to us, while reacting with aggression to other family members. A pet that is a pet only to the owner confers a certain sense of power and exclusivity that may be very pleasant, however undesirable for the parrot and the rights of other family members.

We can see now how our own hidden needs and agendas can create problems for us when we attempt to train and relate to our birds. If we suspect that we ourselves are creating an obstacle to our parrot's progress toward acceptable behavior, we need to be ruthlessly honest in assessing what is motivating our attitudes and make every effort to change them if we decide we're part of the problem.

Discipline

There is a tremendous difference between discipline and punishment. We should *never* physically punish our parrots. They do not understand physical punishment, and such measures will only make the situation worse. The parrot may react with severe aggression. Or, almost as bad, it will become so intimidated and terrified that it may never be able to regain its trust of humans. And from the parrot's perspective, why should it?

A dictionary definition of *punish* is "to subject to pain, loss, confinement, death, etc., as a penalty for some offense, transgression, or fault; to handle roughly or severely." Obviously, a parrot acting from instinct does not realize it has done anything wrong. Even what appears to be a deliberately aggressive act on the bird's part most often has its roots in instinct.

The key is to teach the bird such behaviors are not acceptable and to condition it to refrain from unwanted actions. *Discipline* comes from a Latin verb that means "to teach." This is literally what discipline is about. It means "training to act in accordance with rules; to drill; instruction and exercise designed to teach proper conduct or action."

The operative words in the definition are *drill* and *exercise*. We must be willing to set aside ten to fifteen minutes every day—better yet, twice a day—to work with our parrots to train them. We are willing to do this to obedience train a new puppy; it is no different with the newly weaned parrot just brought home, or the older bird that has acquired bad habits.

We must discipline ourselves, also—to commit to the process, to exercise the necessary patience and gentleness—to accomplish the training process with our birds. We must make every effort to look at the world around us from the parrot's viewpoint and to appreciate what motivates its behavior. We must discipline ourselves to commit to consistency, so that all our good efforts are not wasted in careless moments with our parrots. We must discipline ourselves to refrain from reacting with anger if we receive a nip or if the parrot seems slow to respond to our training. Parrots are intelligent and will react positively to our training efforts, but no miraculous, overnight results are likely. Lasting achievement takes time. Slow is fast when it comes to working with our birds.

The concept of loving discipline is discussed in My Parrot, My Friend, but it bears repeating here:

> We must stop viewing discipline as an unloving element in our relationships with our parrots. Discipline should instead be viewed as ultimate love and respect for a receptive, adaptable, intelligent being that comes from a world of which we know very little, into a world of which the parrot has little knowledge or understanding. Overindulgence and lack of discipline is nothing less than lack of respect for the bird . . . Discipline in the form of guidance and gentle enforcement of behavior limits will not break its spirit. In an atmosphere of properly applied discipline a parrot's spirit will grow and bloom. It is an almost mystical paradox that only in discipline does freedom

exist: freedom to fulfill one's potential, freedom to love and be loved. Discipline is a part of love, and love is a part of commitment.

Discipline and the Previously Owned Adult Parrot with Severe Problems

The material discussed above especially applies to the newly acquired adult parrot with behavior problems carried over from its former home. This will be discussed at greater length in chapter 5. Extraordinary patience, love, and consistent discipline will be necessary to turn around these probably abused parrots.

Disciplinary Guidelines

The famous child psychologist Rudolf Dreikurs established some very practical disciplinary guidelines for use with young children. They can be applied, with some modification, to working with and training parrots. These guidelines are discussed in depth in My Parrot, My Friend. They provide a useful basis for working with our birds successfully, as well as for integrating them into our family lives.

When mistakes happen, don't make a big fuss over them.

**Parrots cannot be expected to be overjoyed by
the attention of strangers.**

- **Be firm without dominating through punishment.**　Parrots, like
children, need limits established for them. Because they are not instinctively equipped to know how to survive and live comfortably in a
domestic setting, they must be taught. Doing so, and enforcing these
limits with devoted discipline, will go a long way toward reducing the
bird's anxiety and making it open to training and interaction with its
human family.

- **Show respect for the parrot.**　No relationship can develop and thrive
without respect. We must respect our parrots for the unique position they
occupy in the animal kingdom, for their intelligence and adaptability,
and for their loyalty. We must have genuine consideration for them and
concern for their physical, emotional, and spiritual well-being. Our
parrots will respond positively to this. In the mysterious way of all good
relationships, we intuit goodwill on the part of the other member of the
friendship. So do parrots.

- **Eliminate criticism and minimize mistakes.**　Parrots are bound to make
occasional behavior mistakes. All humans do, too. Only those no longer
living are immune from committing errors—a rather extreme way to
achieve perfection! When mistakes occur, correct them calmly and

firmly, then go on to your next objective. Our parrots have no idea what we're ranting about thirty minutes after they've "decorated" the sofa or ripped the button from a shirt. You will have wasted your breath. Worse, you will have provided great entertainment for friend parrot, actually reinforcing the unwanted behavior, rather than putting an end to it!

- **Maintain a regular routine for your parrot.**   For a parrot owner, a reasonably flexible routine is a necessary part of life. We know ourselves that when our lives become chaotic—with too much pressure, too little time, and unexpected demands—we become irritable and feel a terrible loss of control. So it is with animals. This is not to say that a routine should be established and followed with a stopwatch. But our parrots need to know within reason when they'll be fed, when they'll be put to bed for the night, when they'll be out of their cages for time with their family members, and when they can expect to experience all the other routine events of their day. Within this loose framework, much variety can be introduced. As long as it is not taken to extremes, our parrots thrive on it, especially when they know that there are "cornerstones" to their day on which they can rely.

- **Sidestep power struggles.**   Parrots are programmed to achieve dominance. Even the most well-mannered parrot will never quite give up this game. When unacceptable dominance behavior is exhibited by any parrot, it should be corrected calmly and firmly. Unless it is ill, the pet parrot must be gently but firmly made to follow reasonable requests— every time. Incidentally, requiring our parrots to pop out of their cages and onto our hands when they're eating, sleeping, or not feeling well is not reasonable. Nor is it reasonable to expect them to react sociably to a room full of strangers, or at a loud party. Respect, remember? That having been said, once the correction is made, do not further engage the parrot with verbal or physical punishment. This will only serve to perpetuate the bird's behavior and increase its drive to become dominant at all costs, because it thinks being number one is the only way to escape more extreme unpleasantness.

- **Make your requests reasonable and simple.**   When it comes right down to it, there are not many behaviors our parrots need to learn in order to live happily with humans. But these behaviors need to be thoroughly learned. Beyond that, complex rules and commands of which a parrot has no concept and will be unable to understand and act upon are a fruitless waste of time. This is one reason that verbal commands need to be short. For example, it is much more effective to say "Up" than "Now honey, get up on Mommy's arm so I can take you out of your cage."

- **Have fun together.**   That's what a good relationship with our birds is all about. Even training sessions can be fun for both human and bird if we make them so. The owner that approaches training sessions with enthusiasm and goodwill sets the stage for the parrot to respond positively and enjoy the praise it receives when it learns and performs well. In fact, training sessions of any kind, whether the parrot is learning the "Up" command, having speech lessons, or mastering a trick, are great facilitators in the bonding process. When you are both really enjoying each other's company and making progress, the fun factor becomes infectious, and you'll find yourselves looking forward to the next session.

What Has Been Learned in This Chapter?

- Lack of understanding about our parrots' true nature is one of the greatest obstacles to training parrots successfully.

- Often, our own attitudes and behaviors must be changed in order to successfully relate to and train our parrots.

- Enabling our parrots to misbehave is a common reason why they do not respond positively to our training efforts.

- Enabling unwanted behavior on the part of our parrots is a problem that resides exclusively with the owner and is often subconscious, requiring honest soul searching to identify and correct.

- Discipline is *not* punishment, but a way of guiding, teaching, and training.

- To be effective, discipline and training must be carried out with love, consistency, and commitment.

- Our training goals often may need modification when working with older parrots that have acquired serious, long-term antisocial behavior.

- The disciplinary guidelines we use when working with our parrots are very similar to those used with young children and are very helpful as training aids.

- Overindulgence and lack of discipline is not a kindness to your parrot, but a lack of respect for it by the owner.

4

The Weanling

Children are what they are made.

—French proverb

What Is a Weanling?

A weanling is simply a young parrot that has recently become independent of its parents and is ready to leave its breeder to live with new human companions.

A weanling parrot has most of the physical skills of an adult bird, *i.e.,* the ability to self-feed, to climb, to fly, and to groom itself.

What it does not have are social skills. If the weanling were wild and had just joined the flock, it would have to begin learning all the social skills necessary to become a successful flock member—in other words, to survive. Many newly weaned birds, including parrots, never live to see their first birthdays in the wild. Disease, predation, and inability to learn survival competence all contribute to heavy first-year mortality.

One of the most valuable responses a young animal of any species acquires is fear—not the paralyzing terror so often associated with fear, but the healthy caution that allows the animal to detect and evade danger. Nature is both ruthless and relentless in teaching this lesson, and those who do not learn do not survive. It's as simple as that.

Weanlings are adorable, precocious, and often quite a handful!

The weanling is different in some ways from its wild counterpart. *It has a beginning level of trust toward humans, and it does not fear them as a wild-caught parrot would.* In fact, it knows no fear whatsoever toward man, beast, or any kind of circumstance. Breeders take great care to rear their chicks in a nurturing, non-threatening environment. This lack of fear in the hand-reared youngster can lead to serious problems later in life, because without proper socialization, training, and discipline, many have no hesitation in attacking a human being overwhelmingly larger than themselves and often do this when displeased or in the throes of the sexual hormonal surges associated with breeding condition.

Those who have had the experience of living with both wild-caught and hand-reared parrots can attest to the fact that the wild-caught birds are far less prone to act aggressively (provided they have been properly gentled and trained) than the hand-reared parrot, who may give a gratuitous nip or bite when its beak is out of joint.

Some breeders are becoming aware of this potential problem, and as a result, we will probably see many parrot chicks being left with their parents through most of the nestling period so that they will have the opportunity to learn to be parrots, with all that entails. This should not mean the weanling will be wild when its new owner acquires it, for the breeder will have taken care to work with the youngster to ensure its tameness before it leaves his or her home. Young parrots are very easily gentled in these circumstances.

The benefit to this practice will be that when the weanling finally comes to the breeder's hand for gentling, it will experience a small, healthy dose of fear: This is a creature with whom it has had no experience, and this fact should create a healthy respect on the parrot's part because it does not quite know what to expect at first. This is in contrast to the parrot that may never have seen another parrot, but only its human surrogate parent from the time it first opened its eyes. I believe the old saying that familiarity breeds contempt may have a great deal of bearing on some hand-reared birds' willingness to behave aggressively at times with human companions.

It is my belief that chicks reared in this way will make immeasurably better companions than those that are currently being hand-reared to create a "superior" pet, or because the breeder enjoys hand-rearing nestlings. Of course, there are times when hand-rearing becomes necessary—when parents won't care properly for them or won't incubate their eggs, or when illness demands treatment for parents or chicks. However, a few breeders are now allowing the parents to do most of the rearing. They have kept track of these chicks and report that nipping and "temper tantrums," which are fairly frequent in young parrots, are not occurring to nearly the degree with those chicks whose parents had the primary responsibility, as opposed to chicks they hand-reared from a very early age.

Other Weanling Characteristics

In addition to the fact that the weanling is predisposed to trust humans and to have no fear of them, it is important to realize that *the young parrot will have no conditioned obedience responses* common to the well-trained dog. We must also understand that in the great majority of cases, *the weanling will not know how to amuse itself*.

Because of this, we must assume the task of not only teaching the necessary social skills the parrot needs, but of providing it the "obedience training" necessary to allow the parrot to become a well-behaved member of the family. We will also need to teach the young bird how to amuse itself during the times it will spend in its cage, not directly interacting with its humans.

Helping our parrots learn to play by themselves is extremely important. Because of the way most parrots are hand-reared, they have little or no experience in exploring and playing with new objects. Some may be downright phobic about them. It's that old "Whatever is new may cause me harm" instinct that's hardwired into their brains as a survival mechanism. This mind set is frequently complicated by the fact that many hand-reared youngsters quite naturally think they are the center of the universe. This is a consequence of the breeder's attention to the parrot's well-being during the rearing period, but it can have far-reaching and unwanted consequences as the bird becomes older, for it may feel abandoned when it realizes it is not receiving the same amount of human attention it did before it was weaned. Not knowing how to play alone and be content doing so can lead to problem screaming, feather plucking or mutilation, and sometimes aggression fostered by a sense of resentment.

Goals for Teaching and Training the Weanling

As owners of newly acquired young parrots, we should have the following goals in order to ensure that the bird has the best possible start in developing its maximum potential as an ideal companion.

- Provide a secure, nonthreatening environment for the bird during the first few days in its new home.

- Establish a loving, firm dominance in a relationship with the bird from the very beginning.

- Establish a daily routine for training, during which the parrot will learn the skills it needs, at the same time building and reinforcing the bond between ourselves and our birds.

- Help the parrot to learn how to play and be comfortable by itself during certain periods of the day.

In doing these things, we must be very aware that our birds have not come to us as ready-made companions, and that it is our job—and ours alone—to help it achieve its full potential as a unique, delightful companion.

The First Few Days at Home

We want our young parrot to feel comfortable and safe in its new home with us. It's exciting to bring home a beautiful exotic bird, one that we may have saved for and looked forward to for some time. It's only natural to want to show it off to friends and family, and shower it with an abundance of attention and love. However, it is a good idea to start as we mean to continue.

It is unrealistic to think that we can continue to give our new parrots as much attention in the coming weeks and months as when it first arrived to start its life with us. It is unfair to the parrot to give it this impression, for, as mentioned earlier, this may lead to problems later on when family members must continue with their routine of work, school, and the business of living. This is really no different from having small children. As much as we love them, we cannot be with them or shower them with attention all their waking hours. We wouldn't even want to, for this would seriously delay their learning and development into responsible, independent adults. So it is with parrots.

Before the young parrot arrives home, prepare its cage by setting it up in an area where it will be able to see its new family members and their activities but will still feel a sense of security when the newness of everything becomes a bit overwhelming. A corner in the family room, or whatever room sees a good deal of activity, is good. However, the cage should be out of the immediate traffic flow. Be sure to avoid placing the cage directly in front of a window, where the direct rays of the sun may cause discomfort or even overheat the bird, or drafts may be a problem.

The day the parrot is to come home, place food and water in the cage ahead of time. One or two safe toys can be included in the cage's decor, but more than this will clutter the bird's living space and may be threatening to it. Remember to line the cage tray with newspaper, too. Avoid corn-cob bedding, as it contains contaminants that the parrot can inhale, creating illness. Cat litter and cedar shavings should not be used either. Be sure to have a sheet or other suitable cage cover ready to use when the bird goes to sleep at night. In this age of central heating, cage covers are no longer needed to keep the parrot warm at night; however, they provide a tremendous sense of security when it is ready to roost. The cage cover also serves to cut down on the visual stimulation the parrot might otherwise experience if its cage is in a room that will be used after it has been put to bed for the night.

A small night light may be in order for the first few days, until the parrot has become familiar with its cage and surroundings and to the night noises in your home. If your new parrot has been accustomed to having a soft toy to sleep with, provide one, making sure it has no parts the bird could pick off and swallow or choke on.

When you arrive home with your new friend, place it in its cage. Speak gently to it and gradually introduce other family members. Leave the parrot in its cage for the first day or two, until some of the threatening novelty of its new situation has worn off and it becomes a little more accustomed to the sights and sounds of its new surroundings. During this period, talk to it softly and frequently during the day. Play soft music for it and gently encourage it to play with the toys you've provided. Be aware of how much the parrot is eating and observe its droppings carefully. Presumably you will have taken the parrot to your avian vet before it even came through the front door, to make sure it is in good health. If you have any concerns during the first few days the bird is with you, do not hesitate to call the vet, the breeder, or both for advice.

Establishing Dominance from the Beginning

By the third day, the parrot should be ready for its first out-of-cage experience with you. This will be your first hands-on experience with your new parrot, and it is very important that the bird understand from the beginning that you are the "flock leader," or "alpha bird." It is therefore important that you, the owner, realize the importance of having the parrot follow through with the intended action—in this case, coming out of the cage when you want it to.

Give the "Up" command. Most youngsters will scramble out onto your hand as soon as it is offered. (If your parrot is of a small or medium-sized species, offer your hand. If it is an exceptionally large Amazon, such as a Mealy, or a very large bird such as a macaw or cockatoo, offer your arm, as it supplies a more secure perching surface.) For those parrots that are bashful, gently persist until the bird steps up on your hand. *It is critically important that you persist until the parrot does as it is asked.* From the beginning, the bird needs to understand that you cannot be manipulated into letting it do what it pleases, such as refusing the "Up" command. Once the bird is securely perched, slowly and gently remove it from the cage. Remember that young parrots are frequently clumsy, so a steadying hand on its back may be necessary.

After the bird is out of the cage and on your hand, move steadily to a chair or sofa and sit with the parrot for a few minutes, speaking softly and reassuringly. Do not allow it to climb to your shoulder and perch there. At this point, the parrot is ready for its first "obedience" lesson, and you may proceed to this step.

These all-important Three Basic Obedience Skills will be discussed in detail in chapter 5.

What If the Parrot Won't Come Out of Its Cage?

Though it is uncommon, sometimes a young parrot will refuse to approach your hand initially. It may do this in a variety of ways. It may hang upside down from the top of the cage or cling to the side of the cage. It may scramble about on the floor of the cage, or it may attempt to lunge and nip. All of this may look

**This parrot is as determined not to exit its cage
as the owner must be to remove it.**

somewhat threatening, but it can be dealt with quite easily. Remember, your primary objective is to allow the parrot to understand that your word is law in such matters. If you allow the bird to refuse your command, it has just learned something very interesting and useful—that it can bluff you and get away with it, thus being left to do as it pleases. The bird will not hesitate to do this again the next time you want it out of its cage.

Toweling is a safe, humane way to remove a reluctant parrot from its cage.

If the parrot attempts to nip as a way to consolidate what it perceives as a defensible position and justifiable attitude, a loud "No" will usually suffice to stop this behavior. If the parrot steadfastly refuses your hand, gently towel the bird and remove it from the cage. Refer to the drawings for the correct technique. Toweling does not hurt the parrot, and it protects the owner from being nipped or more seriously bitten.

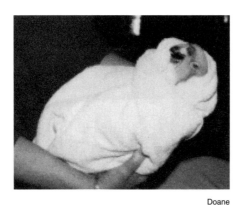

Doane

Doane

Two views of the author's Yellow-naped Amazon, Ollie, correctly toweled and restrained.

Remember to speak softly and soothingly. Don't loose your composure, as the parrot will surely sense this and react negatively. Carry the bird to your chair and remove the towel. Give the "Up" command and offer your hand. The parrot will more than likely be ready to climb up. (Parrots nearly always blame the towel, not the person using it. In this situation, they are very apt to see their human as the "rescuer" from the dreaded towel!) If the parrot is still reluctant to step up, place you hand against its belly with gentle pressure. The bird will then almost automatically step onto your hand or arm.

When the parrot is comfortably perched, praise and pet it. Spend a few minutes getting to know each other a little better. Do not allow it to climb to your shoulder and perch there. Then proceed with the first obedience lesson.

Do I Have to Spend All My Time Training My Parrot at First?

You must spend the time needed to accomplish the all-important basic obedience behaviors, but don't neglect play time. Just make some time every day to be together and enjoy each other. This could be watching television, reading or singing to your parrot, letting it sit on the T-stand near you while you pay bills or talk on the phone—whatever seems fun and natural. Many parrots enjoy being in the kitchen while meal preparations are afoot. However, this should be allowed *only* if the oven and/or range are not in use. Nor should there be pots of hot food or liquid sitting anywhere in the room. Safe activities are mixing batter, chopping veggies, and setting the table—things that do not present any safety hazard for your parrot. Many parrots enjoy being around computers. They seem fascinated by the monitor. As I am now writing, my Umbrella Cockatoo, Miss Molly, is peering at the words flowing across the screen and enjoying every minute of it!

General Guidelines for the Young (or Adult) Parrot

In addition to the Three Basic Obedience Skills, there are several protocols to keep in mind when interacting with your young bird. These protocols, practiced faithfully and in conjunction with the obedience drills, will ensure that the bird becomes a warmly welcomed family member, rather than a disagreeable relative you'd just as soon lock in the attic.

- **Purchase a T-stand.**   Buy one preferably before your bird comes home.

- **Have the parrot's wing feathers trimmed.**   And keep them that way.

- **Don't start routines with your parrot that you will not be able to continue.**   For example, rigid adherence to a certain time every day that is spent with your bird will lead it to expect this come what may. It's better to establish that at some point during the day you will be spending quality time with the bird, but not always at the same time. In this way, screaming tantrums can be avoided.

- **Never allow your parrot to come and go freely from its cage.**   You must always take it out and put it back. This is an important, non-invasive way of letting the bird know you're in charge.

- **Don't allow your parrot to nip or bite, even in play.**   A "little earth-quake" will serve to distract the bird and is unpleasant enough that the parrot will soon learn not to nip. This technique was pioneered by Christine Davis, renowned parrot behaviorist, and is most effective. If the parrot is very young and mouthing rather than nipping, a sharp "No" and distraction with an appropriate toy is an effective way to serve notice that its behavior is not welcome and will not be tolerated.

- **Be very careful about allowing the parrot on your shoulder.**   Until you have lived with your bird for at least three or four months, shoulder sitting should not be permitted at all. This is a position of dominance for the bird and one in which it cannot be controlled. Allowing a parrot to perch on your shoulder too early in the relationship may result in serious injury. Some parrot species are more reliable in this position than others. African Greys are probably the most steady and least likely to bite or nip in a fit of pique. But even with this species, it will depend on the individual. No Amazon parrot should ever be allowed on the shoulder, as they can be temperamental and unpredictable at times.

- **If you decide your bird can be trusted on your shoulder once you have become very well acquainted, you must be the one to place it there.**   Do not let it scramble up of its own accord. Again, you are using subtle dominance that lets the parrot know you're the one in charge.

- **Do not, under any circumstances, allow the parrot to run about on the floor.**   It's dangerous for the bird. You cannot control where it goes or what it does when on the floor. It also can lead to terrible problems with territoriality.

- **Let your parrot sample as many new foods as possible during its first months with you.**   It is important to establish what should become a lifelong pattern of good eating habits. Don't, however, let your bird have alcohol or binge on junk food. Chocolate and avocados, in particular, should not be offered. Both contain substances that can cause illness in your parrot.

Let your parrot sample as many new foods as possible.

- **Don't let your parrot have seed.**   It is high in fat, has virtually no food value, and is the equivalent of letting your children grow up on soft drinks and fries. Serious, irreversible liver damage and early death result from exclusive seed diets.

- **Begin setting behavior guidelines for your parrot from the very beginning.**   No purpose is served by waiting beyond the initial two- or three-day acclimation period, other than allowing the parrot to learn undesirable behaviors that may be difficult to change later.

A Note on Diet

We are what we eat. This applies as much to our parrots as to ourselves. Parrots should have a daily diet consisting of 50 percent pellets, 25 percent fresh or thawed frozen vegetables, and 25 percent fruit. There are many pellets formulated for parrots, but it is best to avoid those made with dyes. In addition, the fat content should be no more than 4 percent for birds other than the large macaws.

It is wise to use a pellet with a reasonable protein content to avoid possible future kidney problems. Bird kidneys are half mammalian and half reptilian in their cell structure. As a result, some birds do not seem to be able to process large quantities of protein without some long-term damage. I personally like a pellet with no more than 11 or 12 percent protein content. The diet of parrots in the wild is probably low in protein, most of their diet being made up of fruits, greens or "milk" seed from various plants, flower buds, and insects. There are probably times when the protein content fluctuates upward, but in irregular spurts, depending on the availability of food sources. It follows, then, that for captive parrots, a year-round diet containing 16 or 17 percent protein is probably not something with which their bodies are equipped to deal.

Some pellets also contain large quantities of various sugars. The content of animal food is always listed, with those in the greatest amount at the head of the ingredient list. Become a label reader! If you see things like dextrose, fructose, and gluconate at the top of the list, pass the product up.

What Has Been Learned in This Chapter?

- A young, newly weaned parrot has virtually no social skills, and it is therefore the owner's responsibility to teach it these skills.

- The weanling has a basic level of trust toward human beings that can be built upon or destroyed by the owner, depending on the owner's motivation to work constructively with the bird.

- The hand-fed weanling has no sense of fear. This lack of fear, and the lack of respect for certain situations it engenders, can create problems for both the parrot and owner.

- The weanling has no conditioned obedience responses and must be taught these by the owner.

- Weanlings frequently do not know how to amuse themselves, to play, and to be comfortable by themselves for extended periods of time. They must therefore be encouraged to develop these skills.

- It is the owner's responsibility to provide a secure environment, establish loving dominance, and set up a regular training routine for the newly weaned parrot.

- The three basic obedience behaviors involving the "Up" command are absolutely essential and nonnegotiable in providing a sound platform upon which other social skills can be developed by the parrot.

- When training a parrot, commitment by the owner is essential if lasting results are to be achieved.

- When training a parrot, the owner must be gently firm; physical punishment and threatening words and tone of voice absolutely must be avoided.

- Make the training sessions fun; let the parrot know you're enjoying the process; end the sessions on a high note.

- If you find yourself becoming angry or out of sorts during a training session, terminate it rather than create a negative situation that may cause the parrot to react in undesirable ways or come to dread its next session.

- With very few exceptions, once a command has been given, the owner must firmly and gently persist until the parrot complies.

- Good nutritional status is necessary for all parrots, regardless of what activities it is involved in. Poorly nourished parrots cannot be expected to learn effectively.

5

The Three Basic Obedience Skills

Practice makes perfect.

—English proverb

Your parrot's mastery of obedience skills is absolutely essential if you expect to enjoy a long, happy friendship together. Whether the parrot is newly weaned, is older, or has marked behavioral problems, obedience training and socialization is obligatory if severe problems are to be avoided. Even for nestlings, it is never too early to begin laying the groundwork for obedience skills that will be learned shortly after weaning.

There are many who will disagree with this, citing their relationships with their own birds and stating they did not formally train their parrots and feel it was totally unnecessary. However, the majority of these owners have young birds that have not yet reached maturity and that are, to a great extent, still biddable and somewhat easy to handle. It is amusing to hear the comments of some of these owners when questioned closely about the nature of their relationships with their birds. Many report that, no, they can't handle the parrot with anything other than a wooden dowel; that, yes, getting the parrot into its cage is a real struggle; that, unfortunately, the parrot tends to be temperamental, so they really don't handle it as much as they should or would like; and that their spouse is afraid of the parrot, or has begun to object strenuously to its vocalization, even though they themselves get along just fine with the bird. One detects the faint but unmistakable presence of the serpent in Eden.

A Cautionary Tale

Just recently, I was visited by a husband and wife whom I have known a number of years. Nine years ago, I helped Larry acquire his large cockatoo—his second parrot. He was eager to learn how to socialize the parrot, as his first had been wild-caught and he had not experienced rearing a domestically bred parrot. We had many talks about how to rear and socialize the bird, including hand-feeding and weaning it, as Larry's new pal was only eight or nine weeks old when he acquired it.

All seemed to go well until I received a call from Larry some months later. The cockatoo was seven months old and "refused" to wean. The truth was, Larry enjoyed the bird's dependency and prolonged the hand-feeding period far beyond what was necessary or emotionally healthy for it. After much struggle—mostly on Larry's part—"Melvin" was weaned. The parrot had no problem with this, as it had been eating well on its own for some time. Larry, a confirmed bachelor with only his two birds and a deep nurturing drive, truly suffered. He daily prophesied Melvin's death of starvation.

This trauma, however, was weathered and, as sometimes happens, we heard only sporadically from Larry over the next four or five years. Then three years ago, our paths crossed again and Larry—the confirmed bachelor—proudly announced that he had met the love of his life and that she and her small dog, Bwana, had moved in with him and Melvin. We met Zoe, and she was a delightful woman whose childhood and adolescence had been spent on her family's farm in Nebraska. She loved animals but had a firm, no-nonsense attitude toward them. She was also a firm disciplinarian.

Our paths diverged once more for nearly three years, until I was called from my office by the doorbell, to find Larry and Zoe on the doorstep with distressed expressions. Could they come in and talk? Of course.

It didn't take much prompting to learn the difficulty: Melvin. He was now nine years old and for the past two-and-a-half years had been making Larry's and Zoe's life unbearable with his nonstop shrieking. The problem was exacerbated by the fact that Larry and Zoe were now working out of their home, and it was no longer possible even to receive or make a phone call because of the noise level. Further, unless Melvin was allowed to perch on Larry's shoulder for hours on end, he became nasty and aggressive. No less than a surgical graft to Larry's body would have satisfied Melvin. Larry said, "I'm a prisoner in my own home. I never knew it could get like this—so bad and so confining. It's impossible for me to live a normal life the way Melvin is."

Attempting to find the cause of the problem, I asked many questions. The answers, though sad, were not surprising.

Shortly after Larry and Zoe had begun their lives together, they acquired a second dog—a high-strung and somewhat aggressive Dachshund. Melvin was suddenly competing with another bird, two dogs, and a spouse for Larry's attention. Further, Melvin had been allowed free flight all over the house for at least eight years. Larry confessed that he was unable to put Melvin in his cage until it was dark. He then turned off all the lights and waited for however long it took for the parrot to amble back to its cage. Needless to say, this had become a terrible burden, especially when the day had been long and hard, and Melvin's shambling progress to his cage at night might take as long as thirty minutes.

Melvin refused to come to Larry's hand. He had begun to bite Zoe. The couple were angry with each other—Zoe because Larry expected her to put up with Melvin's ridiculous behavior, and Larry because he felt Zoe didn't "understand" Melvin's needs. Larry, prompted by Zoe, knew something had to be done, and quickly.

Once again we talked about obedience training. Finally, they left, Larry promising Zoe and me that he would mend his ways and "do right by Melvin" by trimming the cockatoo's wing feathers and beginning obedience training.

However, I was not surprised when I received a phone call at nine the next morning. In strained tones, Larry told me he had decided the best thing for all concerned was to find Melvin a new home. Try as I might, I could not persuade him to commit to working with the bird. Larry began to sob and was forced to terminate the conversation because he was no longer able to speak. Before this, however, he begged me to find a place for his beloved but intractable cockatoo.

With misgivings, I did as Larry requested. When I called to tell him of the placement I had arranged for Melvin, Larry had once more changed his mind and indicated he just couldn't give up Melvin. Two weeks later, I saw him and Zoe again. Larry had not trimmed Melvin's feathers and had not begun to work on obedience training. He said he simply felt it wasn't fair to the bird! The noise level generated by the cockatoo was still unbearable, and Zoe was at her wits end—her husband would neither place Melvin or work with him to make things better.

The very next day, another telephone call from Larry brought me out of the aviary. This time he was sure—he and Zoe had another long talk, and he definitely wanted to place Melvin with another owner. This time, he stuck by his decision. So Melvin was placed with a couple who were experienced with parrots and had worked successfully with another problem individual of Melvin's species. When the day arrived for Melvin to leave Larry and Zoe, Larry was so agitated he could hardly speak, leaving his wife to complete the necessary transfer arrangements with me.

So far, Melvin has settled in nicely with his new owners, and they report a decided decrease in the volume of noise the cockatoo makes. Larry still feels bad about giving up his bird, but is trying hard to convince himself he made the correct choice. There is no doubt that his and Zoe's lives are easier without the never-ending shrieking in their home.

Obviously, there were many factors at work in this case that eventually led to a very unhappy, stressful situation for Larry and "forced" placement of the bird. However, the chief factor was Larry's inability to admit that discipline and commitment for himself and the parrot were necessary from the very beginning. In Larry's view, how could that be? After all, the bird was so young, so adorable, no trouble at all. Larry could not or would not see that the parrot would not always remain so. Nor could he have foreseen the major changes in his life that would act to intensify and escalate Melvin's uncivilized, incorrigible behavior. There was also a certain degree of laziness operating in the situation. Owning and socializing a parrot requires time and effort, which Larry could not be bothered with. He had created a monster and in the end caused himself heartbreak, because he could no longer deal with the problem created through his own refusal to obedience train his bird.

The sad end of Larry's and Melvin's relationship was unnecessary and totally avoidable. Please do not make the same mistake with your own parrot. To use a human analogy, all babies are adorable and helpless. However, without proper upbringing, those adorable babies grow up to become selfish, socially irresponsible, sometimes dangerous adults. It is the same for parrots.

A Note on Training Rewards

Use praise and petting, not food, as a reward. Praise is always handy, whereas food is not. Further, after the initial obedience training away from the chosen training area, it will be very inconvenient to reward with food every time the bird complies with a command. You don't want to turn yourself into a walking cupboard for the next twenty to forty years, after all!

The First Obedience Skill

Content: To teach the parrot to come onto your hand or arm from a T-stand.

Goal: The parrot performs the required action each and every time the "Up" command is given, the action becoming so reflexive so that every time it hears the command, the bird automatically raises its foot without thought or hesitation.

Time Required: Ten to fifteen minutes, uninterrupted, twice daily.

Training Area: A quiet room free of interruption or distraction, such as an unused bedroom or bathroom.

**When the "Up" command is given, the parrot's foot should
raise automatically and reflexively.**

**Establish a rhythm when working your
parrot on and off the training perch.**

Equipment: A sturdy T-stand with the perch at waist height. Such stands may be purchased from pet stores or ordered from bird supply houses regularly advertising in bird magazines such as *Bird Talk*. It is highly recommended that a T-stand be acquired before the parrot arrives in your home so that no time is lost in this very important training step.

Technique: Place the parrot on the T-stand. Place your hand or arm in front of the bird and give the "Up" command. When the parrot complies, praise it and return it to the stand, being *sure* the bird is a little lower than the perch, thus causing it to step up onto it when you give the "Up" command again. Drill continuously for the ten- or fifteen-minute training period, being lavish with praise every time the bird performs correctly. Do not let the parrot refuse your command. Be gently persistent until it performs properly. At the end of the session, praise and pet the parrot and return it to its cage to rest, sleep, eat, play, or do whatever its little birdie heart desires. If you find yourself becoming angry or upset during the session, terminate it. It is better to do this than to create a situation in which the parrot begins to feel angry or threatened in response to your feelings.

Tips: A rhythm should be established with this drill that is almost hypnotic and quite pleasant to the parrot: "Up," praise, back to the perch; "Up," praise, back to the perch. Try not to let the rhythm deteriorate. If the parrot attempts to nip, reprimand with a loud "No." If it attempts to nip while on your hand, a short downward jerk of your arm *each* time this occurs will be very effective in stopping such attempts. Allow your parrot to experience your pleasure and delight in its cooperation. Be alert to signs of tiring, and stop the session before this happens. Some birds will work quite happily for fifteen minutes, others for only ten. The trick is to stop when the bird is still having a good time, so it will look forward to the next session.

When to Proceed with the Next Behavior: You may do this when the parrot automatically raises its foot without hesitation *every* time you give the "Up" command. Progress is an individual thing. Some birds may have the behavior down pat in one week; others may need two or three weeks. However, under no circumstances should the owner spend less than one full week on this drill before moving on. Even after this behavior has been mastered to your satisfaction, review all learned behaviors several times at the beginning of each session devoted to the next steps.

The Second Obedience Skill

Content: To teach the parrot to come onto your hand or arm from the top of the cage on command. It may seem contradictory, as we have already cautioned against allowing your parrot to perch above you. However, at some time in their lives, most parrots will manage to get to the cage top. Additionally, several cage manufacturers build play gyms on their cage tops, although from a standpoint of minimizing aggression, these arrangements are questionable.

However, it is valuable to the bird's development to learn that you are still in charge, even though it may temporarily be "bigger" than you are. This part of the training schedule also teaches the parrot that its cage is not sacrosanct and private to itself—that you, the owner, have every right to command and expect obedience in and around the cage, as well as away from it. This is very important, because some parrots become very territorial around their cages and can act aggressively when in or on them. There is even a school of thought that states parrots can and should be expected to bite if someone reaches into the cage. This

**A well-trained parrot comes to its owner
from the cage top on command.**

is a pure fiction. You would reasonably expect to be able to enter your child's room without fear of physical harm, and it should be no different with your parrot.

Prerequisites: Reflexive, automatic response to the "Up" command from the T-stand. *Do not* attempt the current behavior until this has been satisfactorily and consistently achieved.

Goal: The parrot obeys the "Up" command while on top of its cage—automatically and without hesitation.

Time Required: Ten to fifteen minutes, twice daily.

Training Area: Cage top at a time when household noise and activity are at their lowest level.

Equipment Needed: Cage top, along with a sturdy step stool that will safely and comfortably raise you to a level at which the parrot is approximately at mid-chest or lower.

**It may be necessary to use a sturdy stool to
raise yourself higher than the parrot when you
begin work with the Third Obedience Skill.**

Technique: Remove the parrot from its cage using the "Up" command. Re-view the "Up" command several times using the T-stand. Carry the parrot back to the cage and place it on the cage top. Mount the stool, being sure you are steady and your footing is secure. Offer your hand or arm to the parrot using the "Up" command. When the parrot complies, praise it lavishly and place it back on the cage top. Continue to drill in this manner, establishing the same rhythm you used in the first step: "Up," praise, back; "Up," praise, back. If after two or three days the parrot is responding well, abandon the step stool so that you are lower than the bird (at least with most cages), and continue on with the daily drill without your "perch."

Tips: Let the parrot know you're enjoying its company and its efforts to learn and to please you. Start each training session reviewing the "Up" command from the T-stand. Spend one to two weeks on the current behavior before going on to the next step. Be *sure* your parrot has learned the off-cage-onto-hand drill thoroughly and can perform it automatically *every* time before proceeding to the next behavior. End the session while you're both having fun.

The Third Obedience Skill

Content: To teach the parrot to step onto the hand or arm from within the cage.

Goals: The parrot responds to the "Up" command from any location within its cage, automatically and unhesitatingly.

Prerequisites: The parrot has mastered the "Up" command from both T-stand and cage top.

Time Required: Ten to fifteen minutes, twice daily.

Training Area: The cage at a time when household noise and distractions are at a minimum.

Equipment: The parrot's cage.

Technique: Review previously mastered steps several times before proceeding with the current behavior. After drilling on and off both the T-stand and cage top, return the parrot to the main perch in its cage, remembering to praise it enthusiastically. Do not remove food, water, secondary perches, or swings during this exercise; the object is for the parrot to come to your hand *anywhere* inside the cage. Give the "Up" command and offer your hand or arm. (By this time, the bird's foot should be raising reflexively as soon as it hears this word. If not, go back to the previous two drills until it does.) When your parrot steps up, praise it and remove it from the cage for a few seconds, telling it how pleased you are and what a smart bird it is. Return the bird to the main perch and repeat. Continue doing this for the entire drill period. Establish the same rhythm you used when training the previous two obedience skills. After two or three days, if the parrot is performing well from the main perch, place it on its swing or secondary perch and continue the drill.

Tips: Start each session with a review of previously learned skills. Remember to enjoy the process and let your parrot know you're enjoying it. End the session while both of you are having fun. Once the parrot has learned to comply with the

"Up" command without hesitation from all three locations—T-stand, cage top, and within the cage—drill all three behaviors several times daily. This can be worked into your daily interactions with the bird and need not be done in scheduled sessions such as those during the initial training.

So there we have it: the three basic behaviors using the "Up" command your parrot needs to start it on its way to becoming a *blue-ribbon psittacine citizen!* The commitment you make to following this program regularly and consistently will bring huge dividends as your bird grows and matures.

This little guy has earned his "Good Citizen" award.

Toward the end of training each of the three basic skills, it is very helpful to have another family member (or members) work with the parrot, also. This is especially recommended if others in the household will be providing care for the bird.

One wonderful benefit of structured training periods is the level of bonding and mutual trust that occurs between owner and parrot. Provided the owner has treated the bird with respect and has taken the trouble to make the sessions fun and rewarding, the relationship will begin to deepen and strengthen. This result alone makes embarking on such a program worthwhile, regardless of the very real value of properly training and socializing the bird.

No Vacations

It is important that the parrot be required to follow through correctly every time the "Up" command is given. It makes no difference whether you give the command or another family member does. The bird should never be allowed to refuse the command unless it is ill. Naturally, you will respect the bird's right to eat and sleep without distraction. At other times, barring illness, you must be certain that your parrot complies with your very reasonable request.

What About Slip-ups?

Occasionally, even the best-behaved parrot will refuse a command. When this happens, be sure to observe it carefully to ascertain whether illness is lurking. If you are satisfied that the parrot is merely testing you and the limits you have set, persist until it responds to the "Up" command properly, praising lavishly when it complies. If for some reason your parrot is just being a little stinker for the heck of it, towel the bird gently and set it on your hand or arm. Again, praise the bird extravagantly when it is out of the towel and where you want it to be. The parrot will soon learn that sulks will not release it from its obligation to behave properly. It will also learn that complying with your wishes brings a great deal of pleasant attention—something it craves, enjoys, and will work for over and over.

Sometimes parrots will refuse to comply with commands when there are strange people or animals in the area. Whether to force the issue in such circumstances is always a judgment call. If there is real reason for the bird to feel threatened—for example, a friend who has brought his or her dog along, or the presence of boisterous children—it is probably better to let the bird remain in its cage. This is one of the few times, other than illness, that your parrot can be allowed to "play hooky." (It is always a good idea to drill the parrot on whichever skill you have been temporarily forced to abandon as soon after the incident as you are able to manage.) Otherwise, firmly but gently demand that friend parrot put its best social foot forward and do as it has been asked.

Adult parrots that have never been taught obedience skills are sometimes downright antisocial!

6

Training the Adult Parrot

Age is ripeness.

—American proverb

How should we define the "adult" parrot?

For our purpose, age, although an important factor, is somewhat secondary to the bird's life experience. The adult parrot is well past its fledging (weaning period). It may be a year old or twenty years old. The most important factor is that since leaving the breeder, it has not lived or been treated as a tame bird. This lack of handling will have had the effect of causing it to revert in some ways to "wild" behavior. In addition, it will not have had the socializing of a parrot living with a responsible owner. These two factors will be compounded if the parrot was parent- rather than hand-reared.

It is still possible to acquire a parrot that was legally imported prior to the implementation of the Wild Bird Conservation Act of 1992, although none have been imported into the United States since that time. This may happen if the new owner inherited the bird from a relative or purchases a breeding bird imported before the Act became law. This, however, is not too likely, nor would it be wise. Parrots that have had mates and reared young are seldom candidates for the role of companion animals. The more likely scenarios are that either the

79

owner has purchased a hand-reared parrot that has been in a pet store since the time it was weaned, thus having received minimal handling or socialization; or the individual has acquired a previously owned parrot that its original owners have given up for some reason.

The Adult Parrot Without Previous Owners

Such a parrot will probably have retained some of the trust and comfort level around humans it had when newly weaned, although it may well exhibit a degree of wariness around people a youngster would not. This will make training and socializing it more difficult than if it were just fledged. Basically, the same training regimen applies to the adult parrot in this situation as would to the weanling discussed in chapter 4.

There are two exceptions the owner may have to consider, though. First, the parrot may be reluctant to leave its cage, showing none of the usual eager enthusiasm one sees with a weanling when the owner removes it for training the first time. This is partly due to the parrot's instinctive fear of new surroundings and people. It has had time to develop this instinct free of human intervention, and it has not been modified in any way by the training/socialization process. Second, it may be somewhat more willing to rebuff advances by its new owners by lunging and biting. At this point, its jaws are capable of delivering a painful nip, unlike the younger bird that has not yet acquired full adult strength. Amazon parrots and macaws are more likely to behave with some degree of aggression in this situation than are cockatoos, budgies, cockatiels, *Pionus* parrots, and other smaller parrot species, simply because they are by nature more assertive. African Greys may react with loud growling and an obvious threat posture. But again, these are generalities. Each individual bird is different, regardless of the species. As well, a large, threatening parrot may be more intimidating to its owner than a smaller bird.

Not all domestically bred adult parrots will react as though they believe they are being threatened when first confronted by owners intent on the training/socialization/getting-to-know-you period. However, the owner must be prepared to consider this possible reaction in his or her initial handling of the bird.

Because of this, we need to take the following precautions:

- Learning the proper toweling technique.
- Having the parrot's wing feathers trimmed properly prior to working with the bird.

- Acquiring a sturdy dowel at least eighteen to twenty inches long and of an appropriate diameter for the parrot's feet.

- Being thoroughly familiar with the techniques involved in teaching the three basic obedience skills.

It will be the owner's task to decide how willing the parrot is to be handled, and to tailor the approach accordingly. In any case, once the initial settling-in period has passed and the time has arrived for hands-on work with the parrot, one should always approach the bird with cheerful confidence and a loving but firm attitude about the training process.

The Settling-In Period

This is the interval after the parrot first arrives home. As with the weanling, the cage and its furnishings, including food and water, should be in place so that the bird can go directly into its new quarters upon its arrival. Two or three safe, appropriate toys can be provided, but do not clutter the cage. For one thing, too many toys dangling about will crowd the parrot's living space. Second, by rotating toys one or two at a time, the bird will not become bored and indifferent to them.

As with the weanling, place the cage in a protected corner or against a wall to create a sense of security. Do not place it directly in front of a window, not only for protection against drafts and direct sun, which could seriously overheat the parrot, but because theft of valuable parrots is a thriving business. For the sake of security, the world at large should be unable to see your costly parrot sitting in its expensive cage in the living room picture window. It's an open invitation to disaster.

Let the parrot remain in its cage, observing the household and its routine, for at least two or three days. Provide a good, nutritious diet. Speak softly, gently, and often to the bird. Play soothing music, and guard against boisterous onslaughts from children and other family pets.

Use this period to determine as much as you can about the parrot's personality. Does it relish attention, or is it shy and easily startled? Does it solicit attention by climbing on the cage wires and bowing its head for a scratch, or does it exhibit threat posture when you or other family members approach? Does it get as far away from you as possible, clinging to wires at the back corner of its cage?

You can learn a great deal about how to tailor your training program to the bird by observing. Regardless of the parrot's behavior when you approach, maintain a calm, cheerful attitude and remember to speak kindly even if your new parrot growls or shrieks at you. Above all, do not retreat if the parrot threatens.

Stand next to the cage, your hands at your sides, and continue to speak soothingly. Do not leave until you are ready. The parrot must not assume that you can be gotten rid of by a show of cowering, screaming, or making threat postures.

At this point, it is probably a good idea to consider the owner's posture. Move slowly, as parrots can be frightened by abrupt movements and gestures. Do not wave your hands in front of the bird's face, or lean over and point at it. A person leaning over, head extended, arms out, and hands waving, looks remarkably like a parrot in attack mode; and this is exactly how most parrots interpret the situation: You are a huge featherless creature intent on starting a fight.

With those parrots that will accept treats from the hand, the offer of a favorite tidbit three or four times a day will go a long way toward convincing the bird that it has reached the equivalent of birdie heaven. Parrots have been fed by their parents or the breeder and will feed and accept food from their mates. Take advantage of this point of parrot etiquette to gain its trust and help it understand your intentions are honorable and good.

A word of caution: Let the treat come only from your hands or those of a family member. Once you've decided that a grape or an apple slice, or whatever, is the parrot's favorite, don't put it in the food bowl, available whenever the bird wants it. Let the parrot begin to look to you for this delicacy. And be sure the treat is healthy and nutritionally sound: no chocolate or junk food—and no seed. Whatever the offering, it should be given only two or three times a day in very small quantities. Otherwise, you risk ruining the parrot's appetite for its regular diet. Obesity can result from treats—even fruit—if they are overdone.

The First Obedience Skill

The adult parrot should go through the same basic training program the weanling does. This is explained in detail in chapter 5, and you should review this thoroughly before commencing work with your bird. Once you are well into the program, you will not need to consider or use any special technique. The first time you must take the parrot from its cage may require a bit more finesse on your part if the bird is reluctant to come out on your hand—which is by no means rare. Also, the first few training sessions may require the use of a wooden dowel as a temporary perch in lieu of arm or hand.

Before removing the parrot from its cage, be sure your T-stand is set up in a room where there will be few if any distractions. Once the parrot is out of the cage, you will want to proceed directly to the training area.

Getting the bird out of its cage the first time can be stressful and a little frightening for the owner, as well as for the parrot. It's the first time you will have handled the bird, and you really don't know until the time comes whether it will

**The untrained adult parrot must also learn
the Three Basic Obedience Skills.**

obligingly step onto your hand, try to give you a hard bite, or hang upside down from the cage wires, screaming as if it is in imminent danger of being killed. The only thing you know for sure is that somehow, the bird must be humanely taken from its cage. It is only natural to be a little nervous about how best to accomplish this.

Open the cage door, offer your hand or arm, and, in a firm voice, give the "Up" command. Do not command in a tone of voice that the parrot may choose to ignore because it sounds like "baby talk." You need not sound angry or harsh, just firm. You want the parrot's attention, and this will get it. When the parrot steps up, praise it lavishly and withdraw it from the cage in a steady, gentle motion.

For those birds who refuse to come onto your hand, it is tempting to open the cage door and wait for the parrot to emerge on its own. While this may seem on the surface to be humane and nonthreatening, you will have taught the parrot

Removing from the cage an untrained adult parrot whose tolerance for handling is unknown can be a bit frightening at first.

from your very first attempt to interact with it that it can frighten you away, leaving it free to come out or stay in just as it pleases. It will have achieved the first round victory of "Who's going to be top parrot?" in your home.

Toweling the Parrot

If a reasonable attempt to take the bird out on your hand is not successful—or if you honestly fear a nasty bite—calmly close the cage door and get your towel. Before toweling the parrot, remove food and water dishes, dangling toys, and swinging perches. Depending on the cage, you may also want to remove the perches. All this will make it much quicker and easier to towel the parrot and swiftly remove it. This procedure should not be drawn out any longer than necessary. Do not be afraid that the bird will hate you for all time. It won't. Parrots blame the towel, not the person wielding it.

Before toweling the parrot, be sure you understand how this is done. Use a regular-sized hand towel, not an oversized bath towel or beach towel. It helps tremendously if the towel is not so thick you can't tell the bird's head from its tail once you've grasped it. And remember, do not clamp your hands around the bird's chest or abdomen. Birds have no diaphragm and breathe with the muscles of their bellies. If you restrict these muscles, you can actually suffocate the parrot.

Remove all food dishes and swinging toys and perches from the cage prior to catching up the parrot in the towel. Open the cage door and, taking the towel in both hands, reach in and gently grasp the parrot with one toweled hand, just behind the head and around its neck. Do not worry about choking the bird. Un-like mammals, parrots have cartilage that encircles the entire windpipe, making it very difficult to cut off their air supply by firmly holding it around the neck.

Once the parrot's head is secure, grasp its feet with your other toweled hand. Gently loosen its feet from the perch or cage wires. You may also have to manipu-late its beak from a similar "death hold." Withdraw the parrot from its cage and cradling its body against yours in a football hold—being sure its head is adequately restrained—use your free hand to wrap the towel around its body. You may also want to loosely cover its face.

The entire procedure may take as long as ten minutes the first time. As your skill increases, you should be able to remove the parrot using this technique, in a matter of minutes. With regular, daily training sessions, use of the towel for this purpose will eventually be unnecessary. However, all parrot owners should be able to towel their birds quickly and skillfully. Toweling is absolutely essential when trimming flight feathers and nails. It is also essential to be able to restrain a sick parrot for a trip to the veterinarian and to administer medication.

The First Obedience Skill, Continued

With the parrot on your hand or arm, or in the towel, proceed to the training area, remembering to speak soothingly as you go. If it jumps to the floor, reach down and offer your hand or arm, giving the "Up" command. If the bird starts the equivalent of the hundred-yard sprint in the parrot Olympics, retrieve it, using the towel if necessary.

Upon reaching the training area, place the parrot on the T-stand for a mo-ment, allowing it to regain its composure and view its surroundings. Remember to praise your parrot when placing it on the perch, so it learns to associate the T-stand with pleasant experiences. If the bird should jump down, calmly retrieve and replace it. Do this as often as you must. The bird cannot be allowed to "play hooky" from its lessons.

Begin the First Obedience Skill outlined in chapter 5. If the bird becomes angry and aggressive, you may want the bird to step up on the dowel rather than your hand. In addition, if you are feeling rather shaky and unsure of yourself, perhaps fearing a bite when you offer your hand or arm, the dowel is very useful. It will lower your anxiety level, which is communicated to your parrot and affects training response. Second, you will avoid teaching the parrot to fear stepping up on your hand or arm. This particularly unfortunate result occurs because parrots very often use their beaks to steady themselves when going from perch to arm and back; inexperienced owners easily confuse this use of the beak with the parrot's intention to bite. They reflexively jerk their hand or arm away, and the confused parrot doesn't know how to respond. As a result, the next time you give the "Up" command, the parrot will reasonably be reluctant to oblige. A moving, unsteady perch with no security is something no bird willingly chooses.

So until you are completely comfortable and trust the parrot not to bite—or the bird climbs onto the perch at your command with no show of aggression or discomfort—offer the dowel rather than your hand or arm. As the parrot becomes more and more proficient and comfortable stepping up onto the dowel, gradually decrease the distance of your hand to the bird's feet, until it is actually stepping onto the hand that is holding the dowel. Continue drilling the bird in this manner for a day or two until the response becomes so automatic the parrot doesn't notice when you finally cease using the dowel and start offering your hand instead.

At this point, you and your parrot should be well on your way to successful mastery of the first obedience skill. You will both be feeling more confident and secure with each other. As this feeling takes hold, start incorporating some play time together, always making sure the parrot follows through on your "Up" command. Don't forget to praise your parrot lavishly each time it performs correctly. And do remember to make all training sessions fun for you both, ending on a high note so your bird will look forward to the next session.

The Second and Third Obedience Skills

After a minimum of two weeks working on the first obedience skill—providing your parrot has mastered it—you may start the second. Both the second and third skills should be drilled twice daily for ten to fifteen minutes a day, for two weeks each. Do not proceed to the third skill until the first two have been successfully mastered. And always remember to start each training session with a review of previously learned skills.

The Previously Owned Problem Parrot

Bird lovers are, almost by definition, animal lovers. As such, many of us find ourselves taking in a parrot someone else wants to give up because the bird has behaviors the original owner cannot tolerate. Sometimes, we come across mistreated parrots and our hearts go out to them. Can we not bring them home? At this point, we ask ourselves, "What can I do to rectify the problems and give this parrot a decent quality of life?"

Working with a previously owned parrot with problems can be a challenging but rewarding experience.

It sometimes happens that the new owner is not aware that the parrot has problems. The bird's previous owner may not have mentioned them at all in his or her desire to be rid of the bird and its problems. Many times, the new owner brings the parrot home and the bird behaves charmingly for the first days or weeks, only reverting to problem behavior when it begins to feel secure in its new home. This is particularly frustrating and puzzling for the current owner.

In many cases, these birds have developed their antisocial behaviors over a period of years, and it will take a great deal of time to wean them to more accept-able ways of relating to people and/or learning to be happy and comfortable in their own skins. The parrot may be a flesh or feather mutilator. It may scream incessantly. Or it may bite aggressively and indiscriminately.

Sometimes these parrots will never become ideal pets. When this happens, we have to make the decision whether or not to accept the bird for what it is. Is it happy? Does it seem content with the level of sociability it has managed to ac-quire? Can we be happy with this?

When we ask ourselves these questions, we need to weigh our own needs against those of the parrot. If we are satisfied that the bird's quality of life is much improved over its previous circumstances, then perhaps we will be comfortable accepting and enjoying the parrot for what it is, rather than mourning its lost potential as a confiding pet. Naturally, we want close relationships with all of our pets. But on the other hand, the love and mercy that prompts us to improve an animal's life will prevail—even if our relationship with it is very different from what we had envisioned. There is a great deal of satisfaction in providing a "hurt" parrot with a safe haven and the best life you are capable of giving it. The parrot will know at some level that you are its friend and, to the limited extent it is able, will trust you. A bond will forge almost in spite of the circumstances—a different one perhaps than might have been expected, but one that nevertheless will have its own rewards and triumphs.

Training the Previously Owned Problem Parrot

With problem parrots, the settling-in period is more important than with untraumatized birds. If you decide the bird's problems are beyond your ability to modify, for your own safety seek the help of a qualified professional parrot behav-iorist. Large parrots have powerful beaks and are capable of inflicting serious dam-age when angry or afraid. You must consider your own safety, as well as the parrot's potential for increased quality of life.

If, on the other hand, you feel you can work successfully with the bird, the same training regimen that applies to weanlings and previously unowned adult birds applies to the problem parrot—even more so. Many of these parrots have never learned to accept loving dominance from a human. Perhaps they simply did not have the benefit of proper training or socialization, or they may have been mistreated. Older parrots in breeding condition that have never been trained or socialized are particularly challenging.

Use the settling-in period to wean the parrot to a healthy diet if it was poorly nourished in its previous home. It is very important that such a bird have a thorough physical examination and diagnostic blood work during this time. This is even more critical if the parrot exhibits poor plumage, regardless of what previous owners may have told you. Psittacine beak and feather disease is fatal and can be diagnosed only by a qualified avian veterinarian. This disease is discussed in detail in *The Parrot in Health and Illness* (New York: Howell Book House, 1991).

After the initial settling-in period, commence working with the first obedience skill, proceeding to the second and third skills after the first has been *completely* mastered. Expect that each skill will take at least two to three times longer with an older, problem bird than with a weanling or a previously owned parrot. In addition, be sure to review the general guidelines for parrots in chapter 4 and follow them. Be particularly aware of avoiding situations in which the bird may act aggressively, such as allowing it to perch on shoulders or above your head.

It is important that you develop empathy—a sense of what the parrot is experiencing as it learns to give up old, inappropriate behavior and relate acceptably to humans. It is hard for us to function following loss of control in our lives and personal circumstances. Such loss is even more difficult for a parrot, programmed to equate dominance with its very survival and instinctively battling for that dominance.

The "Time-Out" Area

When working to modify the behavior and retrain/resocialize problem parrots, a "time-out" area is a necessity. In fact, a time-out area is useful in any case. This is a small cage (or a roomy carrier, for a small parrot) without toys or other cage furnishings, other than a perch. This cage or carrier should be placed in an isolated part of the house and the parrot placed there for no longer than ten minutes at a time, as a disciplinary measure when it indulges in major antisocial behavior. This is a noninvasive, nonaggressive method of discipline that utilizes a technique the parrot understands and avoids if at all possible—isolation from its "flock."

When using the time-out area, you must do so with consistency. Every time the bird misbehaves, it gets ten minutes in the time-out cage. It is important that you do not speak to the bird when carrying it to and placing it in the cage. Leave the room and shut the door. Do not linger to tell the bird how naughty it has been. Do not make eye contact or in any other way "reward" the parrot with your attention. Be sure to set a timer for ten minutes, so you don't forget to retrieve the parrot. Not only is it inhumane to leave the bird in this situation for extended periods, but after the ten-minute time limit, the parrot will no longer associate the disciplinary measure with the infraction. Further, it may start to scream for attention, a behavior you do not inadvertently want to teach.

Problem Behaviors: Screaming

It is normal for parrots to do a bit of morning and evening vocalization. This may last as few as three or four minutes, or as long as ten or fifteen minutes. Parrots having large vocabularies may talk incessantly rather than scream during these times. Even parrots with limited vocabularies may repeat

"Time out" for Polly!

the few words they know over and over. Of course, some parrots may not vocalize during these usual times, choosing instead to shout and talk at intervals throughout the day. It is also normal for parrots to yell along with the vacuum cleaner, the sound of running water, or music they particularly like—or dislike.

Some parrots are naturally quite noisy, especially those with good talking ability. The same drive to communicate in "parrotese" allows them to become talented talkers. In this case, you really can't have your cake and eat it, too, especially with respect to the Amazon species.

Other parrots are spurred to great communication heights by television programs. Most adore a dramatic chase scene and enthusiastically chime in with the blaring sirens and emotional background music. Others, like my husband's favorite buddy, J.B., have their favorite sports teams. J.B. loves to watch football games, but he particularly likes the Chicago Bears and seems to be able to distinguish them from any other pro football team. I'm sure this is because he picks up on our excitement when we watch our team. Alas, sometimes J.B. cheers "his" team with such fervor, he has to be banished to another room so we can hear the plays!

J.B. and his family love watching the Chicago Bears.

Many parrot owners—myself among them—report that their birds love to yell when they are on the telephone. This is probably in response to the owner's voice, to which the parrot has a natural instinct to respond. It is also probably an attention-getting device. Parrots are perfectly capable of knowing the owner's attention is directed elsewhere when he or she is on the telephone. This behavior is very much like that of small children who often do the same thing. And beware! Just like very small children who pick the times their parents are distracted to get into mischief, parrots may do the same thing if they are out of their cages and unsupervised for a period of time.

All parrot owners simply learn to tolerate these normal vocalizations. After a time, one barely notices them, believe it or not!

Last, but not least, it seems that parrots love the sound of their own voices and simply vocalize because they love to do so. It's music to their ears, even if it's not to ours. When you've had enough of this kind of "music," the parrot can often be coaxed to cease and desist by distracting it with a toy, spending a few minutes just talking with it in low, gentle tones, or moving it from its cage to the play gym or some other area the bird likes and that will put its mind on another track.

Problem screaming, though, is an entirely different matter. Basically, this type of vocalization can be classified into four varieties:

- Fear screaming or growling.

- Imprinted screaming.

- Screaming of sexual maturity and breeding condition.

- Perseverant screaming.

General guidelines should be followed with the screaming parrot, regardless of the cause of screaming.

- If the screaming is unexpected and unusual for the bird, the time of day, or the circumstances, or if the screaming itself is "different" in some way, *do* check to make sure the parrot has not hurt itself or become entangled in cage wires or a toy.

- Never shout or yell back at the parrot in an attempt to get it to be quiet. First, it will only cause it to scream louder. Second, the bird may begin to think of it as a game it wants to continue for entertainment value. And third, because you have responded with attention—your return vocalization—you will have rewarded the parrot for its screaming.

- If you know your parrot well, and it understands the meaning of "No!" uttered in a sharp, commanding voice, you may want to try doing this. If the parrot stops its commotion, wait a few minutes so the bird will not interpret this as a reward for its screaming, and provide it with a distraction such as a play gym session or some time on its T-stand in the area near you. *However,* if this doesn't seem to work, don't do it. The last thing you want to do is teach the parrot it can get your attention and play the "I can shout louder than you" game. If this seems to be the case, ignore this suggestion and follow the other guidelines.

- Do not hit the parrot for screaming—or for any other reason.

- Do not bang the side of the cage, shake it, or otherwise manipulate it in an effort to obtain peace and quiet. The parrot will not understand cause and effect. It will become frightened and may learn to become aggressive.

- Do not put the parrot in a dark room or closet for protracted periods. This is cruel and will eventually interfere with your bird's physical and emotional health. It may cause it to scream all the louder in an effort to reestablish contact with its "flock."

- Do ignore the screaming. Giving the parrot no reinforcement for its behavior will have the effect of diminishing the behavior when the parrot finds it cannot gain attention in this way.

- If the screaming escalates to the unbearable, use the time-out cage or carrier for *no longer than ten minutes* at a time. Covering the cage for ten or fifteen minutes may have the same effect, though not usually.

- Remember to praise the bird when it is being quiet. A few kind words and a small tidbit of one of its favorite treats will go far in conditioning the bird to remain reasonably quiet. In this way, you are rewarding for *wanted* behavior rather than unwanted behavior.

- If at all possible, provide variety within the routine of your parrot's day. Boredom leads to a great deal of preventable shrieking. If the television has been on for a period of time, turn it off and play some music or an environmental CD. If the bird has been playing quietly in its cage for a while, maybe a play session or a trip to the office (if you work at home) is needed. Maybe it's time for a trip to the play gym near a window, or a training session. Or perhaps your parrot would enjoy a change of scene by "helping" you prepare dinner. Be creative within the limits of safety and your available free time.

Fear screaming or growling usually has obvious sources. Sometimes it is difficult to know why the parrot is frightened, and therefore hard to solve the problem in order to stop the screaming. If the source of the parrot's discomfort and fear is obvious, it can be removed. Sometimes it may be necessary to move the cage so the offending object can't be seen. Sometimes we may not be able to find the problem. When this happens, we must be willing to experiment, even though we ourselves may not be able to detect the cause of the fear and resultant screaming.

It is common for parrots to be afraid of new toys. Sometimes we bring home what we think will be a real treat for our birds, only to find them cowering and yelling in the corner of the cage, trying to get as far away as possible from our newest love offering. We may feel a little rejected when this happens. The answer is to introduce any new toy gradually, especially if it is larger than the bird, very colorful, or has a lot of "stuff" hanging from it—dangly things, multiple strands of knotted rawhide, or similar attachments. Before hanging the new toy in the cage, lay it on a nearby table for a day two so your parrot can see it won't jump up and eat it for lunch. When it comes time to hang the new toy, you may want to hang it on the outside of the cage for a few days before moving it inside. Gradual introductions like this are far less threatening than sudden ones, and a good deal of unpleasantness for both of you can usually be avoided.

**It's common for many parrots to be afraid of
new toys, especially ones bigger than they are.**

Some parrots scream with fear at anything new. Some even scream in fear
over people and objects with which they are familiar. When parrots react in this
way, the best course often is to help them confront the problem in a supportive,
gentle, but firm manner. The parrot may learn its fear is irrational, having nothing to do with actual circumstance. In any case, it would be a mistake to let it
think there is *really* anything to be afraid of. With parrots that tend to be highly
phobic, it would only serve to limit its world at a time when you're trying to help
it learn to be more comfortable and at ease.

A further note about sources of fear screaming: Some wildlife programs contain material showing hawks and owls flying or swooping on prey. These can be a
source of real apprehension for parrots. Again, this is an individual response. But
if you should find yourself in this situation, turn off the television, calm the bird,
and return it to its cage. Just think how you would feel if you thought that critter
was real and was heading toward you, looking for some easy pickings!

Imprinted screaming has two sources, both working together to produce the problem. It always occurs in hand-fed parrots unwittingly reared by the breeder and, later, by the owner, to feel they are the center of the universe. Birds like this usually do not know how to amuse themselves, expecting their owners to be the equivalent of a full-time entertainment director. When they become bored or want attention that is not forthcoming, they begin to screech for it. In short, they are spoiled, and it is our doing. The importance of teaching our parrots how to amuse themselves and be content without constant attention by their owners cannot be overemphasized.

We can start this important habit by allowing the parrots time alone in their cages, without our interference. When the parrot is in its cage, we can provide a selection of safe toys that can be rotated two or three at a time every week or so. We can play the television, stereo, or radio for them. We can place the cage so that even though we are not with them constantly, they can see and hear the household activity. It is also very important to praise the parrot when it is being content and quiet, doing its thing on its perch or play gym or in the cage. It is hard to overestimate the positive effect of words of praise, a comment in passing, or an occasional scratch on the head now and then to make the parrot feel secure and included. In this way, the parrot does not feel ignored or neglected and is usually happy to go about its business until training or play sessions are due. It may be possible to position the cage so the parrot can see out the window without being subjected to direct sun or the full view of passersby.

The screaming of a mature parrot in breeding condition can be very trying. Usually, once the hormonal surge is over and the bird reverts to nonbreeding condition, the frequent, often ear-splitting vocalizations abate to more normal levels. Not all parrots in breeding condition scream like this; it can be very much a trait of the individual. Early, effective socialization and reasonable owner attention often serve to lessen unwanted decibel levels in the mature parrot. Also, the bird totally at ease with its owner often doesn't feel the need to defend its "territory" by screaming, lunging, or biting. Following the general guidelines for controlling a screaming parrot are helpful. However, such screaming is largely instinctive, and one may just have to grin and bear the worst of it, realizing it will abate with the close of the breeding cycle and a measure of household peace will then be restored.

Perseverant screaming is perhaps the most difficult screaming problem to deal with. Fortunately, the problem is not widespread. In this situation, screaming is constant and for no apparent reason. Often, it is difficult to understand how the bird can even draw breath. There is no known cause. Physical problems such as central nervous system damage could be a factor, or there may be deep-seated psychological difficulties the owner and veterinarian may or may not be able to uncover and treat.

The first step is a thorough examination by a qualified avian veterinarian. Physical illness must be ruled out or, if present, treated. Medications used for people with emotional problems sometimes help, but they are not the preferred approach for a parrot with perseverant screaming. Everything relevant to the bird must be carefully examined: environment, diet, relationships with other family members and pets, manner of handling, and any change in routine that may have triggered the behavior. Changes should be made when indicated, in addition to the physical examination and required blood work, cultures, and X-rays. If medication is prescribed, it must be given as directed. Avoid the temptation to skip the occasional dose or otherwise tamper with the treatment schedule. If follow-up laboratory work is required, be sure it gets done.

Problem Behavior: Chewing

Many owners report their parrots chew up everything in sight. Undoubtedly, a parrot can wreak maximum havoc on your most cherished possessions in an instant. However, in every case, the owner is to blame. As with so many other aspects of living happily and comfortably with a parrot, the wise owner is guided by the admonition "Don't provide opportunities." Parrots should never be left alone and unsupervised out of their cages. They should never be allowed to roam the floor or permitted anywhere determined to be off limits. Chewing is instinctive parrot behavior, but distinguishing between its own toys and a priceless antique breakfront is not.

A gentleman I once met asked me how to keep his Sun Conure from sitting on and damaging a particular lampshade. Amazingly, he was totally sincere and obviously at a loss to prevent this "problem." I told him, "It's very simple. Don't allow your bird near the lampshade." In amazement, he responded, "But how do I stop him? He can fly wherever he likes." We then discussed trimming wing feathers for safety reasons, more thorough bonding, and generally making life more livable with his parrot. I referred him to some area veterinarians who could trim his bird's wings properly; he was thrilled and amazed at the simple solution to his problems. He just had never thought about it.

The point is that we often never stop to think what we're doing. As a result, our birds and our relationships with them suffer, and often prized possessions are destroyed. This works against developing warm feelings toward our parrots and is so easily avoided. Simply *do not give them the opportunity*. We are responsible for our birds, not they for us. Owners must establish and enforce limits, so chewing is not a bird problem. It is an owner problem.

Many owners have a problem with parrots chewing everything in sight.

Problem Behavior: Biting

Most parrots will bite or nip occasionally at some time. This becomes problem behavior only if it is improperly handled. If the parrot learns it can establish dominance by means of threat behavior, the situation may escalate to problem proportions. *True problem biting involves frequent, regular attacks, especially involving the drawing of blood.* Frequently, this kind of biting targets not only those the parrot considers peripheral to its life, but its "significant other" as well.

Following are the most common causes of biting:

- Ill health
- Fear/self-defense
- Excessive or rough handling
- Displacement
- Dominance
- Sexual maturity
- Food solicitation or exploration of their environment by newly weaned youngsters
- Occasional irritability

Several of the above causes are not necessarily serious and can be easily dealt with.

With **biting due to illness,** the parrot typically will not have a biting history. The bite is usually unexpected, can be painful, and leaves an owner wondering why such a sweet bird would do this. This kind of bite should be a red flag, and the wise owner will pay particular attention to the number and quality of the bird's droppings, its appetite level, and its general demeanor. Any departure from normal activity or loss of appetite is a cause for concern. Sometimes the symptoms of illness don't emerge until a day or two following a biting incident. If a parrot acts sick following an uncharacteristic bite, it should promptly be taken to a qualified avian veterinarian.

Fear biting usually responds well to the immediate removal of the object, person, or circumstance that caused it. If the parrot has become deeply traumatized, it may take some time to regain trust for its surroundings and people. This is especially true of abused parrots. Patience and firm, gentle training plus ample time will usually allow the parrot to begin feeling safe with people again. Use of the wooden dowel as the initial perch in the first obedience skill is of great help in working with these parrots.

Occasionally a parrot will experience episodic screaming and thrashing incidents that appear to have no outward cause. When this happens, a thorough examination by an avian veterinarian and appropriate treatment, if indicated, is vital. The parrot may be suffering from a central nervous system problem. African Greys are extremely prone to low blood calcium levels and may have seizures resembling a bird in extreme terror. This condition, *hypocalcemia,* is life-threatening and must be treated as a medical emergency.

The parrot that **bites in response to rough or excessive handling or teasing** will stop when the owner adjusts his or her behavior. Every parrot keeper has at some time accidentally bumped a tender blood feather or prolonged a cuddling session past the parrot's tolerance, only to have the parrot respond with a sharp warning nip. No harm is done by such occasional incidents. It is when the bird is continually subjected to inappropriate play and handling that it becomes a habitual biter in self-defense.

Pinching fingers to **elicit feeding by the owner or simply to explore** is very common with newly weaned youngsters, as noted in chapter 2. Consistently discouraging this behavior and distracting the parrot with a toy, walking it around the room, or placing it back in its cage for a time should prevent this kind of nipping from becoming a problem. The "little earthquake" technique is also very effective. If the parrot nips while perched on your hand or arm, a sharp downward motion will temporarily upset its balance—a very unpleasant though harmless sensation for the bird. When doing this, do not also scold the parrot. Scolding would be providing attention. Turn your head from the bird without even making eye contact—a surprisingly effective technique.

Biting triggered by displacement, dominance, or sexual maturity tends to be a more persistent and serious matter in living with the pet parrot.

Displacement biting, where the parrot cannot reach the object of its displeasure, causes it to bite the nearest person. A sharp "No!" followed by ten minutes isolation in a cage or carrier, consistently enforced, can be very effective in stopping such behavior. The "little earthquake" technique, described above, also works well. Often displacement biting is triggered by the presence of a person the parrot considers a rival for a favorite's attention. In these circumstances, spouses or any other members of the household—including children—often become targets.

As removal of the opportunity for misbehavior is a cardinal rule when handling parrots, the human object of regular, serious displacement biting may wish to refrain from handling the parrot when its "rival" is present. This is only a matter of good, common sense. For example, before he had a mate, my huge Green-winged Macaw, "Eli," was a very affable fellow. Very docile with me when he joined our home, I did not realize his good nature did not extend to other humans.

Eli was destined to join my breeding program, but because I had not yet located a suitable mate and his history was so sad, I allowed him out of his flight while working in the aviary. Because my husband, Bill, helps in the aviary only on weekends, I had no idea that Eli was a psittacine "pit bull." The first time Bill came into the aviary to help after Eli's arrival, Eli jumped from my lap and charged across the floor, beak agape and aimed for the poor fellow's Achilles' tendon. Wisely, Bill left the aviary promptly; I retrieved Eli, returning him to his flight. In this case I was not the object of displacement biting but could have easily been. After that incident, Eli was never allowed out when Bill was in the aviary. It saved everyone considerable grief and pain.

Providing another classic example of displacement biting is "Gizmo," a Timneh African Grey. At six months, Gizmo's owners, Gayle and Pete, brought home an unweaned Black-capped Caique. One evening soon thereafter the whole family was around the kitchen table, Gayle with the baby in her lap, Gizmo on the table, and Pete at the other end deeply engrossed in a TV program. This was to be a supervised get-acquainted session for Gizmo and the new baby. Unfortunately, the Timneh was seized with a severe case of sibling rivalry and charged the little Caique. Gayle put up a finger and uttered a loud "No!" Gizmo stopped in his tracks, shot Gayle a filthy glare and repeated her warning. He then turned, ran to the other end of the table as fast as he could, and sank his beak into Pete's arm. Gizmo was duly reprimanded and put in his cage to contemplate the wages of sin, leaving Pete rubbing his arm and plaintively asking, "What did I do? I was just minding my own business."

Another technique that works well with a displacement biter is having the "rival" establish a separate relationship with the bird. This is an approach upon which both parties must agree. The rival must commit to work with the parrot regularly and consistently. Eventually, the bird may cease regarding the rival as such and will instead begin to relate to the person as a friend. Before deciding on this approach, be sure it will yield the desired result. Much will depend on the parrot's general demeanor and personality. Mature parrots can be very aggressive about protecting a favorite person and may never learn to abandon this behavior. *Never use this method when a child is involved.* The risk of serious injury to the child is far too great.

Dominance biting can be serious. Never allowing the bird higher than mid-chest, except when in its cage, is absolutely necessary. Keeping the wing feathers trimmed is also essential. The sharp "No!" followed by a ten-minute stay in the time-out spot *every* time the bird bites can be used to good effect. Avoiding situations that tempt the parrot to bite is a cardinal rule with the dominance biter. Do not allow the parrot free access to and from its cage; you must place the bird where you want it. Doing so will be considerably easier after the Three Basic Obedience Skills are mastered. The need to work with such a bird until it has successfully mastered these behaviors cannot be emphasized too strongly. Use of the wooden dowel rather than your hand or arm when starting to teach the First Obedience Skill is highly recommended. It provides the all-important sense of security you, the owner, will need to work with the habitual biter.

Obedience skill training is one of the most effective methods available to instill reflexive respect for your commands in the dominance biter. Working through these skills to the point of mastery—especially when used with the other suggestions—will do more than almost anything to stop dominance biting. As with any parrot training, the owner must be committed to seeing the program through to successful completion. When working with a dominance biter, the object of any corrective program is to permanently establish yourself— humanely and noninvasively—as flock alpha. Depending on the individual bird's temperament, you may have to drill and reinforce these skills every day of its life. With some parrots such rigorous drilling may not be needed, depending on the bird's response to you and its surroundings as it spends more and more time in the lovingly dominant environment you have created for it. There is no rule to govern this aspect of living with a dominance biter. Your own knowledge of your parrot's personality, responses, and potential willingness to refrain from dominance biting as your relationship progresses are the primary considerations.

Biting at sexual maturity is related to dominance biting in that the parrot perceives the humans it lives with as potential threats to its territory, which in the wild is likely to become its nesting area. The weanling that comes to its owner as a youngster, having received the benefits of obedience training and proper socialization, will be less apt to act out the aggressiveness of sexual maturity. For these parrots, the tendency to nip or bite should be curbed firmly and immediately, using the methods already discussed.

It is probably wise to refrain from handling the parrot with impunity until the peak of seasonal hormonal activity is past. Do handle your parrot, but also respect its signals and give it more time to itself during the period. When you handle the bird, do so when it is relaxed and unconcerned about protecting the nest. Be especially alert for signs of restlessness and aggression, and return the parrot to its stand or cage before an incident can occur. Never allow a bird, no matter how tame, on your shoulder when it is in aggressive breeding condition.

If you recently acquired a previously owned parrot that has come into breeding condition, it may prove wise to put off starting obedience skills training until after the breeding season is past. In my experience, such parrots do not respond well to new owners when experiencing hormonally mediated aggression. These birds seem to be in their own little world, which nothing penetrates until the drive to establish territory and mate has passed. One can almost see the inward, rather glazed expression in the eyes of some of these parrots. This, of course, makes it very difficult to get and keep the bird's attention for the duration of a training session. Some may enjoy the sessions, responding well in spite of their hormonal state, while others will not. The owner's judgment takes precedence here, but if in doubt, delay skills training until the parrot can enjoy and benefit from the sessions. However, once this happy state is reached, do not delay. The sooner mastery is achieved, the happier for all when the next breeding cycle arrives—and arrive it will, with monotonous predictability.

In summary, parrots bite for many reasons, some transient and easily dealt with, others more serious and requiring active, regular human intervention. But no matter what the reason for biting, the potential for *any* kind of biting can be greatly reduced when the parrot has successfully mastered the Three Basic Obedience Skills.

Occasional irritability is usually very temporary, and the parrot usually responds well to a little time to itself. It may not have slept well. Breakfast may not have been to its liking, or perhaps a favorite food was not provided. Perhaps you have not been spending much time with your parrot for the last day or two and it feels irritable as a result. Parrots are intelligent, emotional beings and can have an occasional bad day just as we do. Be sure to watch for signs of illness, though. As mentioned before, any behavior change can be an early warning sign of trouble brewing.

Problem Behavior: Feather Picking and/or Mutilation

Of all parrot problem behaviors, none is quite so distressing and lamentable to us as the beautiful bird that rips out its plumage or severely damages it. Although parrots are universally loved for many reasons, and for most of us the inner bird is as important as the outer one, still, one of the reasons we enjoy parrots so much is the opportunity to revel in their great beauty. Further, as many feather problems may have a partial origin in psychological causes, we often feel guilty. Perhaps we think we did something wrong, that we failed to take proper care of our parrot, when it behaves this way. Like the parents of children with physical or emotional problems, we may have read all the right books and done all the right things, only to find our bird hideously featherless or worse. It's only natural to ask "How could this have happened?" or "What did I do wrong?" It is also natural to feel angry at the parrot with a problem we somehow were supposed to foresee and prevent.

However, we cannot predict the future. Sometimes in spite of our best intentions, things go wrong. Sometimes remedies are available; other times they are not. In the latter case we must learn to accept what we cannot change. Most people find this very difficult, because our society teaches us that there is a solution for every problem. This is not always true, especially with the plucking or self-mutilating parrot.

Some things we would normally take for granted
may be frightening for our parrots.

Sometimes the cause of a feather problem is obvious. In a wonderful seminar, Christine Davis told of a beautiful Umbrella Cockatoo whose owners had moved it to an adjacent room for the night because the room where the parrot usually lived was being painted. When they looked in on the bird the next morning, to their horrified disbelief, a completely naked cockatoo, with a pile of feathers on the cage bottom, greeted them. They called Ms. Davis for a consultation and sure enough, there was a very obvious reason for the cockatoo's extreme behavior. In the temporary room, on a wall close to the cage, was a chiming clock that boomed out the half-hour all night long. Strange room; dark night; loud, unfamiliar, insistent noise—no feathers.

Very often we simply don't know what causes an apparently normal bird to suddenly remove or shred its feathers or actually chew holes in its flesh. In most cases, the cause will have many factors, among them environment, nutritional level, training and socialization, genetic and hormonal factors, general health, the parrot's relationship to family members, and the existence of other pets in the home. The possibilities are endless. One thing we do know is that once a parrot begins mutilating its plumage, it is often very difficult to stop the behavior. It seems to be a self-engrossing activity, repetitive and stereotypic in nature. As such, it may be soothing for the parrot, perhaps like chronic nail biting or "crib rocking" in young, hyperactive children.

Whatever the cause, or causes, the first thing to do with a plucking or mutilating bird is to get it a thorough veterinary examination. At the same time, the owner and everyone in the household should try to isolate any recent changes or stresses in the bird's life that could have triggered the problem. This is important to the veterinarian making the medical evaluation. When seeking those triggers, remember that what we may discount as a source of stress may be perceived differently by the parrot. For example, a cage placed to give a view from a window may allow the bird to visualize frightening images—shadows from tree branches, a stalking cat on the ledge, and the flight of wild birds all have the power to unnerve.

The second task is to correct as many of the circumstances that could have precipitated the feather problem as possible. If one or two major factors have been identified as probable causes, it may be relatively simple to correct them. If many factors seem to be at work, then, of course, corrections will be more involved and complex. Start with the most obvious and proceed from there.

New toys that are both safe and appropriate, selected to distract the bird from feather mutilation, should be provided. There are many excellent toys available for this purpose, many with multiple strands of knotted rope or rawhide. A new, unused whisk broom works very well to distract the picking or plucking parrot. They give somewhat the same sensation as stripping a feather but, of course, without the same dreadful result. Drinking straws cut to four- or five-inch lengths also seem well-received by parrots with a penchant for feather mutilation. Stick cinnamon, dried pasta, and chunks of fruit and vegetables hung on "skewers" especially made for parrot cages also work well. Millet sprays can also be very helpful, and since they are very low in fat will not cause birds to gain excess weight. Many parrots spend hours picking out each tiny seed—time they might otherwise have spent chewing on their plumage.

The third thing we must learn to do in the presence of a plucking parrot *is to furnish no feedback whatsoever when the bird indulges in this behavior in our presence.* This is very difficult to do in view of the natural tendency to scold the bird caught in the act of removing or damaging its feathers. However, doing this focuses attention on the parrot, and it soon learns that it can draw attention at any time by simply ruining another feather. The time to pay attention to the plucking parrot is when it is *not* damaging its feathers. The kindly word, a scratch on the head, a favorite tidbit—all give the bird needed attention when it is being "good." For the fortunate owner, the parrot eventually learns that none of these pleasures will be forthcoming while it behaves "badly." In some cases, feather destruction may then slow or stop altogether.

Some veterinarians recommend stockinette "body socks" for affected birds. Some parrots accept these well and will wear them long enough to allow feathers to regrow fully. Sometimes, this enforced period during which the parrot cannot reach its feathers to pick or pluck them is enough to break the destructive cycle. Max, my Mollucan Cockatoo, wore such a body sock and tolerated it very well. He has never plucked another contour feather since the sock was removed, although he still clips flight and tail feathers. Other parrots will not tolerate a body sock and will rip it off as soon as it is slipped on.

Elizabethan, or "E," collars are also used by some veterinarians to prevent the parrot from reaching its feathers. I personally feel that these collars do more harm than good. They markedly restrict the parrot's ability to move comfortably and freely and make it very hard for it to reach food and water containers with ease. Weighing the emotional damage they may do against the benefits of decreased feather mutilation, the risk hardly seems worth the benefit.

Some work is being done using herbs to supplement traditional treatment regimens for feather mutilators. Valerian and Saint John's Wort are two such herbal preparations. Valerian acts as a very mild relaxant; Saint John's Wort is a mild antidepressant. Owners may want to consult with their avian veterinarians about the possible benefits of these herbs. These, or any herbal preparation, should never be used without a veterinarian's supervision.

It would be misleading to paint a rosy picture for the full recovery of the habitual feather mutilator. This is one of the most frustrating, difficult things for owners and veterinarians to face. So much depends on the owner's commitment to helping the bird stop the behavior, the bird's personality, and the ability of the owner to remedy or modify any factors that may have caused the behavior. Feather destruction of short duration usually responds better to efforts directed at getting the parrot to give up the behavior. Parrots with long-standing, chronic feather mutilation problems may never give up the vice, regardless of treatment and methods employed. These parrots possibly decrease the behavior, or give it up altogether for a period of time, only to re-commence when some new stress or physiological condition appears in their lives.

We must bear in mind that even the most determined feather plucker is not any less the bird it was before the behavior started. Although it may be not nearly as pretty, it will still have the same endearing traits it had before and should be no less lovable and precious. We should not judge these birds' worth based on shining, flawless plumage. Sometimes the best presents come in amazingly plain packages!

What Has Been Learned in This Chapter?

- There are two kinds of adult parrots: those with and without previous owners. Often the previously owned parrot shows serious behavior problems. Either bird may have been hand-reared or wild-caught prior to the Wild Bird Conservation Act of 1992.

- Regardless of any behavior problems, successful mastery by the adult parrot of the three basic obedience skills is imperative as a basis for establishing a good working relationship between parrot and owner and resolving any problems that may exist.

- The settling-in period for the newly acquired adult parrot is critical for allowing the owner to develop a feel for the bird's personality and attitude toward its family and surroundings, thus allowing for tailoring the most advantageous approach to training and acclimation.

- The owner's posture and gestures, as well as tone of voice and attitude, are extremely important in determining the successful outcome of the work done with the adult parrot.

- When working with parrots, it is important to understand that the beak is used for steadying when the parrot climbs on an arm or hand. This action should not be misinterpreted as an attempt to bite.

- Some previously owned problem parrots will never become ideal pets. This requires us to readjust realistically our expectations for such birds.

- If the owner has real fears and doubts about the safety and advisability of working with an aggressive adult parrot, the services of a qualified parrot behaviorist should be sought.

- It is important to develop a sense of empathy for the behaviorally challenged adult parrot as it learns more acceptable behavior and gives up its habitual dominance and control.

- Providing a "time-out" or isolation cage or carrier is essential when working with the problem parrot.

- Normal parrot vocalizations must be accepted by the owner.

- Problem screaming includes fear screaming or growling, imprinted screaming, the screaming of sexual maturity and breeding condition, and perseverant screaming.

- There are general guidelines to be followed with the problem screamer, regardless of the cause of the screaming.

- The cardinal rule in working with parrots to prevent or modify problem behavior is "Don't allow them the opportunity to misbehave."

- Parrots should never be allowed out of the cage unsupervised, nor should they be allowed anywhere the owner does not wish them to be.

- We, as owners, are often to blame for problem behavior in our parrots because we frequently don't realize that our actions may be contributing to the establishment of these behaviors.

- We are responsible for our birds; not they for us.

- Problem biting involves frequent, regular attacks, especially where blood is drawn. Of all the biting behaviors, displacement, dominance, and the biting of sexual maturity are most serious, requiring ongoing behavioral modification.

- The object of basic obedience skills training, as well as other techniques to socialize and train or retrain parrots, is to establish humanely and noninvasively the owner's "alpha" position within the mixed-species "flock."

- In the case of the previously owned parrot in full breeding condition at time of acquisition, it may be wise to postpone obedience skills training until the bird has reverted to non-breeding condition.

- Causes for feather picking/plucking or mutilation are effectively unknown. This behavior probably has many causal factors and requires the joint efforts of avian veterinarian and owner to correct or modify the problem.

- In the feather-mutilating parrot, it is necessary for the owner to make a detailed inventory of any and all suspected causes for the parrot's behavior.

- We must give feather mutilators no feedback whatsoever when we observe them damaging their plumage. We must, instead, ignore the behavior in order to avoid teaching the parrot it can get our attention by indulging in feather destruction.

7

Bringing Up Baby

The adult looks to deeds, the child to love.

—Hindustani proverb

All young creatures, be they human babies or parrot nestlings, need love. But love is not enough. If it were, avian veterinarians everywhere would not be seeing dead parrot nestlings, brought to them by frantic, well-meaning owners lacking even the most basic information about caring for baby parrots.

The myth perpetrated on the buying public is that if the prospective owner buys an unweaned parrot, it will bond more closely with the owner, thus becoming a better pet. Some even go so far as to state that the bird should be taken home before its eyes have opened, thus facilitating the imprinting process. Some bird species, notably ducks and geese, imprint on the first object they see after they hatch. However, there is absolutely no data to support this with parrots.

Obviously, the newly hatched parrot forms a bond with its parents. We must remember, though, that this is only the first relationship to occur in the parrot's life. It is genetically programmed to loosen this first bond as it prepares to fledge, just as human adolescents seek to loosen family ties as adulthood approaches. The parrot is also instinctually driven to seek and bond with a mate, perhaps for life, after it leaves its parents' extended care. This means it will bond as readily

Some birds, such as ducks, will imprint on the first thing they see when their eyes open. Parrots, however, have better sense!

with a human—*after* the weaning process is complete. This has often been true with those acquiring a weaned parrot youngster and has always been true for anyone fortunate enough to be allowed to share their life with wild-caught birds. The point is that it is totally unnecessary to acquire an unfledged nestling in order to have a close relationship with a pet bird.

This chapter will cover how to care properly for the parrot baby that was purchased before weaning. The primary goal for the owner with an unweaned infant is to keep it alive and healthy. Otherwise, training and socialization become moot.

It is common for many breeders to sell unweaned babies directly to new owners, or to pet stores that may or may not finish the hand-feeding and weaning process. This practice is fraught with difficulties and potential disaster. Although the mechanics of hand-feeding may appear simple, especially with the baby approaching the weaning stage, many things can go wrong—things the owner is usually unprepared to handle. Commonly compounding the difficulties is the fact that many new owners do not establish contact with an avian veterinarian as soon as they acquire the baby parrot. When things begin to go wrong, it is often hard to find expert help in time.

Weaning is a very stressful time for the baby, and it takes great skill to get many parrots through this period while maintaining acceptable weight and health. It is far better to buy a weaned youngster, thus allowing the breeder, who has far more experience and expertise than the new owner, to guide the bird successfully through this process. Relying on pet shop personnel to give advice is chancy at best, as many owners of unweaned babies have found to their regret.

However, if owners of unweaned parrots use the material in this chapter as they complete the hand-feeding and weaning processes, their chances of keeping a parrot baby alive and well should be greatly increased.

Getting Started

When we undertake the rearing of an unweaned baby parrot, we need both equipment and knowledge. We must also make a sizable time commitment. Both these issues will be discussed as the chapter proceeds.

There is one piece of equipment I believe the owner of a nestling *must* have, no matter who or how many individuals may disagree: an *electronic gram scale*. It should be equipped with a basket and a perch. A baby bird's weight gain or loss can be accurately gauged only by such a scale.

Knowing the nestling's progress or lack of it cannot be accurately determined in any other way. In the vast majority of cases, the first sign that something is going wrong is failure to gain weight, or actual weight loss. Because we are dealing with very small animals, this is not something that can be "eyeballed." An accurate gram scale is the only reliable measure. True, there are those who have managed to rear healthy youngsters without a gram scale, in spite of their cavalier attitude. However, many nestlings that are lost every year might have been saved if their owners had known early enough that problems were occurring. It cannot be emphasize enough how important it is to be safe rather than sorry when it comes to your infant parrot's life!

If you are considering buying an unweaned baby, or have already done so, ask your avian veterinarian for sources of good gram scales. Many avian supply companies also stock these, and many advertise in national bird magazines such as *Bird Talk*. These scales are not cheap. A reliable scale in the medium price range will probably cost around 100 to 150 dollars. But considering the price of domestically bred parrots, it is wise to purchase equipment that will best help maintain the bird's health, as well as protect your considerable investment in a pet you hope will be with you for many years.

There is a right and a wrong way to weigh a chick. The right way is to weigh first thing in the morning, *before* the day's first feeding. An accurate daily weight record must be kept, along with the chick's age, the number of daily feedings, and the amount of food taken. The following simple chart is one I have found useful. For the computer literate, this data can be entered on a spreadsheet. However, I urge owners to keep the chart handy in the nursery area, where it can be filled out immediately at each feeding. It is all too easy to delay going to the computer with little scraps of paper. This commonly results in the loss or unavailability of important data should it be needed.

Table 1: Sample Daily Record for the Unweaned Chick

Chick's Name: Chick's Hatch Date:	
Date: Age in Days: Weight: Feed #1:Time/Amount in CCs Feed #2, 3, etc., as above	A standard 8×11-inch sheet of paper will hold enoughblocks for six days' worth of data, will allow room for important comments.

**All parrot nestlings have the same basic needs,
which their surrogate parents must meet.**

All nestlings have the same basic needs:

- Adequate rest.
- Ambient temperature suited to the chick's age and degree of feathering.
- Adequate nutrition.
- Environmental enrichment.
- Gentle, confident handling that gives the chick security.

The basic signs of impending health problems are:

- Failure to gain weight, or actual weight loss, unless the chick has entered the weaning phase.
- A crop that fails to empty completely between feedings, especially if it remains partially full overnight.
- A crop that feels "doughy" when empty and rolled between thumb and index finger.

- A baby that has lost its normal pink color and/or feels cool to the touch.

- Lack of feeding response when the crop is empty and it is feeding time.

- Continual whining and restlessness.

- Beak deformities or splayed legs.

- Change in quality or consistency of droppings.

Any of the above signs, singly or in combination, should be brought to the attention of the avian veterinarian immediately. Chicks are extremely delicate, have very small body mass and immature immune systems, and can "crash" in just hours. The rule of thumb is "If you think something's wrong, it undoubtedly is." Do not delay calling the veterinarian in the mistaken belief that "It's nothing, it will probably go away." It won't, and you may wind up with a dead chick.

It is never too early to begin using the "Up" command. Each time the chick is removed from the brooder (or weaning cage, if it has progressed to one), say to the chick in a kind, firm voice, "Up," as you remove it or lift it up. The chick will become accustomed to the command and the associated action while very young, which is wonderful early training, and this will make the formal training and socialization process much easier when the baby "graduates" to "big parrot school!"

It's a big day when the nestling weans and graduates to "Big Parrot School!"

It is very important for owners to be aware of the *stages of growth* and the associated physical, mental, and intellectual aspects nestlings experience. It helps a great deal to know, for example, if certain activities herald the impending weaning stage, or when the baby is ready to be removed from its brooder to a weaning cage. I will, therefore, spend a little time delving into these important growth stages. Although chicks go through several distinct stages prior to fledging and independence, I will concentrate on the last two, as most owners (one hopes) will have purchased a baby with its eyes and ears open and at least a fair amount of feathering.

Stage I (the Post-Hatch Stage) is concerned primarily with nutrition and rapid growth. It is rare that the owner of a nestling parrot will ever be involved with a newly hatched baby.

Stage II (the Preliminary Stage) involves the development of comfort movements as well as accelerated growth toward motor control and independence. In the early phase, ears and eyes will open and down growth will be heavy. In the late phase, pin feathers will begin to show, and a fear (startle) reflex may develop. This is a natural occurrence, and the owner of a chick in the late phase of Stage II may be surprised to see his or her baby back away when approached in the brooder, or struggle when lifted from a solid surface. It may also hiss or shriek. Sudden bright lights or noises may elicit the same response. This startle reflex is probably instinctive, providing the nestling parrot in the wild with some defense against nest predators. Feedings for a chick in the late phase of Stage II will probably number four a day. The chick will still need a heated brooder. Although most owners will not have acquired a chick in the early phase of Stage II, many also bring home chicks in the late phase.

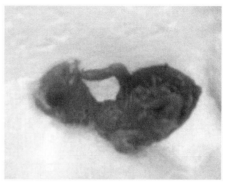

Cole

This day-old Jardine's Parrot is completely helpless. All of its needs must be met by its parents or the breeder.

Stage III (the Transitional Stage) involves the chick's physical and emotional maturation. It will remain awake for long periods between feedings. The chick's time is usually spent playing, observing its surroundings, preening, and practicing motor skills. Feedings usually number two per day. The chick will begin to exhibit self-feeding behavior consisting of picking at the brooder substrate. As soon as this occurs, beginning weaning foods should be introduced for the baby to play and experiment with. Good choices include Cheerios; Wheat Chex; popcorn popped in a hot-air popper with *no* oil; finely diced apple, pear, or broccoli; shredded carrots; frozen corn kernels,

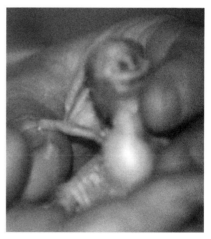

Cole

The same Jardine's baby at four days of age. Note the position of the filled crop in proportion to the rest of its body.

thawed and served at room temperature; and small parrot pellets. Be sure to change the soft food offerings two or three times a day to avoid spoilage. *Do not* introduce the chick to seed. Seed has no part in the daily diet of a parrot and should be used only as a very occasional treat for the *adult* bird or as a reward when trick training.

Cole

The same Jardine's baby at seven days of age. Note the increased amount of down and the huge eye orbits. At this point, the baby's eyes are still closed, as are its ears.

The chick will not become self-feeding for many weeks, so the owner should not expect it to acquire any nutrition from these offerings. Nevertheless, it is extremely important to the eventual weaning process to offer these foods as soon as self-feeding behavior is evidenced. If this is not done, you may find that when the time comes, the chick is in earnest about weaning and the process is lengthier and more difficult than it would be otherwise. Feathering will be well advanced. The chick will be able to walk well and will begin to learn to climb. It will also learn to balance and perch during this stage. The startle reflex will diminish and may disappear altogether. Chicks in this stage will now be able to regulate their body temperatures and will no longer need a heated brooder. It is during this stage that the chick can be moved to a weaning cage. At this time, the young parrot may need only one feeding per day; others may still require two, morning and evening. Appropriate weaning food and fresh water must be available at all times. It is during the last part of this stage that chicks begin to lose

Cole

A four-week-old Hahn's Macaw in the Preliminary Stage.

their "baby fat," sleeking down in preparation for flight. Gradual loss of a few grams per day over a period of a week or two should not give cause for concern unless other danger signs are present.

Most individuals purchasing an unweaned baby will have bought a nestling in the Transitional Stage.

Stage IV (the Locomotory Stage) is the last stage, during which the nestling achieves the independence of flight. As soon as this happens, the owner *must* have the bird's wing feathers trimmed. Feathering will be complete, and the youngster will be completely self-feeding. During this time, vegetables and fruits can be given in larger pieces, and new offerings such as grapes, oranges, bananas, and a greater variety of vegetables can be provided.

Cole

This seven-week-old Congo African Grey is about halfway through the Transitional Stage.

Because the newly weaned parrot chick appears in most respects to be an adult, it may be tempting to think of it as such. This is a mistake. The chick knows very little about how to get along in the family setting, and training and socialization are of utmost importance and should not be omitted. It is appropriate and wise to start the first of the Three Basic Obedience Skills as soon as the chick is perching well. This may be at the end of Stage III or shortly after complete motor independence has been achieved in Stage IV.

The following charts provide owners of unweaned chicks with guidelines on average weights at various stages, average pre-weaning peak weights, average weaning weights, adult weights, and average day weaned. These are only guidelines. Each chick is different, and its progress should be measured within the context of its behavior, alertness, and motor activity as well. However, a chick that is far below the average weights given, or is refusing to wean weeks after the average wean date, should be seen by an avian veterinarian.

Table 2: The Unweaned Cockatoos

(All weights given in grams)

Species	Peak Pre-Weaning Weight	Weaning Weight	Adult Weight	Approx. Day Weaned
Umbrella Cockatoo	At 9 Weeks 492–679	At 14 Weeks 404–589	440	104
Mollucan Cockatoo	At 10 Weeks 759–885	At 14 Weeks 686–826	850	
Bare-eyed Cockatoo	At 7 Weeks	At 14 Weeks 289–385	350 260	80
Med. Sulphur-crested Cockatoo	At 7 Weeks 463	At 14 Weeks 408		
Goffin's Cockatoo	At 7 Weeks	At 14 Weeks 304	350 260	

Table 3: The Unweaned Macaws

(All weights given in grams)

Species	Peak Pre-Weaning Weight	Weaning Weight	Adult Weight	Approx. Day Weaned
Blue and Gold	At 8 Weeks 927–1064	At 14 Weeks 826–922	750	98
Scarlet	At 8 Weeks 931–1072	At 14 Weeks 800–932	900–1000	98
Green-winged	At 10 Weeks 1185	At 14 Weeks 981	1000-1200	100
Hahn's	At 6 Weeks 160–170	At 8 Weeks 140–150	135–150	59
Military	At 8 Weeks 760–1039	At 14 Weeks 768–820	900	91
Yellow-collared	At 7 Weeks 280	At 14 Weeks 248	Approx. 250	70

Table 4: The Unweaned Amazons

(All weights given in grams)

Species	Peak Pre-Weaning Weight	Weaning Weight	Adult Weight	Approx. Day Weaned
Yellow-naped	At 7 Weeks 556–654	At 10 Weeks 484–491	480	77
Double-yellow headed	At 6 Weeks 388–565	At 10 Weeks 352–476	Approx. 450–500	77
Yellow-fronted	At 6.5 Weeks 390–485	At 10.5 Weeks 382–450	Approx. 380–480	77
Blue-fronted	At 6 Weeks 376–470	At 10 Weeks 320–357	350	71
Lilac-crowned (Finsch's)	At 6 Weeks 309–370	At 10 Weeks 279–301	300	70
Red-headed (Greencheek)	At 6 Weeks 314–401	At 10 Weeks 286–319	300	70

Table 5: The Unweaned Africans

(All weights given in grams)

Species	Peak Pre-Weaning Weight	Weaning Weight	Adult Weight	Approx. Day Weaned
Congo Grey	At 8 Weeks 547	At 9 Weeks 538	500	58
Timneh Grey	At 9 Weeks 300	At 12 Weeks 270	320	89
Senegal	At 5 Weeks 146	At 8 Weeks 116	125	56

Figures in the above tables derived from the following sources:

- *Parrots in Aviculture: A Photo Reference Guide*, Rosemary Low; Silvio Mattacchione & Co., 1992.
- *Proceedings of the Seminar on Breeding Psittacines in Captivity*, January 29, 1989, Avian Research Fund; Alamo, California.

- *Psittacine Aviculture*, Richard M. Schubot, Kevin J. Clubb, Susan L. Clubb, DVM; Avicultural Breeding and Research Center, 1992.
- *The Large Macaws*, J. Abramson, B.L. Speer, J.B. Thomsen; Raintree Publications, 1995.
- *Jo's Exotic Birds*, Jo Cole.
- *Flying Colors Aviary*, Gayle Soucek.
- *Trinity Mark Aviary*, Bonnie Munro Doane.

We now consider the unweaned chick in the last two stages of nestling development, what we need to know in order to provide the care to meet the needs of developing parrots during these stages, and the equipment they require.

The Sparsely Feathered Baby (Transitional Stage)

At this stage, a chick is, to all intents and purposes, helpless. Our responsibility is to provide all of the baby's needs: nutrition, warmth, appropriate housing, rest, appropriate playthings and environmental enrichment, and careful, accurate observation on a daily basis in order to avoid problems or rapidly correct any that arise. This is a tall order, and perhaps you didn't fully realize this when you first brought home your stubbly bundle of joy.

If you are fortunate enough to have gotten your baby from a breeder, then you will (or should) have the benefit of his or her advice. However, the avian veterinarian is the final authority, whose advice must be followed regardless of what the breeder may say in a conflict. Those who have purchased their babies from a pet store will not usually have the benefit of the breeder's advice and support. This makes it doubly important that you contact an experienced avian veterinarian *before* you bring baby home.

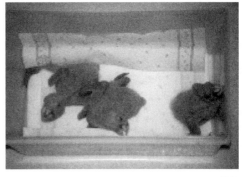

Cole

These Orange-winged Amazon chicks are three weeks old and still in the Preliminary Stage.

Most stores (and breeders) will give a two- or three-day grace period in which you will be able to take the chick to the vet for a checkup and necessary lab work, the agreement being that if anything is wrong, the baby can be returned for a refund. *Do not* neglect to do this. Not only will the baby have the benefit of a thorough physical exam by a qualified professional, but you will have made the first, all-important contact with the most valued ally in your ongoing task of keeping that precious chick healthy. It is a great comfort to know that at eleven o'clock at night (parrots never seem to get sick during office hours!) you can contact your veterinarian's answering service and be recognized as a client when your medical advisor receives your message.

So much for the preliminaries. Now, let's consider "nursery furniture" for Baby Polly. This is very important, because *suitable housing allows us to supply proper warmth for the chick.* Remember, chicks at this stage of development cannot regulate their body temperatures efficiently, so the surrogate parent must do this. In the nest, the hen does this when she broods her chicks. In our homes, we must provide an artificial brooder as an external source of heat, as well as an appropriate, easily cleaned "crib."

Ten-gallon aquariums are highly recommended as a brooder for medium-sized parrots during this stage. For large birds such as macaws and the white cockatoos, a twenty-gallon size is appropriate. A screen lid, used when the aquarium houses reptiles, is absolutely necessary.

Pine shavings or a product called *Yesterday's News®* are recommended as bedding material. *Yesterday's News®* consists of pelleted, recycled newspaper and is the best choice for macaws, as they frequently attempt to eat pine shavings, resulting in serious problems. Another good choice is soft terry toweling, especially if your little one (like some macaw chicks) shows a tendency to nibble on shavings. The toweling provides a soft, graspable surface that works well to minimize sprawling when the chick begins walking. However, toweling must be changed and laundered daily. Do not use cedar bark or shavings: Cedar is toxic when ingested. No corn cob bedding should be used, either, as it harbors harmful fungus. Cat litter is also unacceptable as bedding, nor should you use paper towels or newspaper. Although these materials provide great convenience for the owner in terms of cleaning time and ease, they do not provide enough support for the chick's developing legs and feet and may contribute to causing splayed legs.

Heat should be supplied by a heating pad placed beneath the tank. For best results, a towel should be folded and placed between a *heat-proof surface* and the heating pad. On top of the pad, another folded terry dishtowel should be positioned. Alternately, for an older chick, the pad can attach to the outside of the cage (with a buffer of towels). The chick can then cuddle up to the side of the tank or move away, depending on the temperature. The heating pad should never be turned higher than the medium setting. Observe the chick carefully. If it holds its wings away from its body and breathes open-mouthed, it is too warm. On warm spring days and hot summer days, the heating pad may not be needed at all, although the low setting may be necessary at night unless the ambient night temperature is very high. If your home is air conditioned, the low or medium setting will be needed regardless of warm weather. If the chick feels cool to the touch, is huddled in on itself, seems sluggish, and/or has a slightly decreased feeding response, then more heat should be provided. No exact rules can be stated concerning keeping baby parrots at exactly the right temperature for comfort and physical health. It is a matter of observation, for which the owner must take responsibility.

Cole

One of the Orange-winged Amazon chicks from the previous photo, now six weeks old. Note the degree of feathering, wide-open eyes, and alert expression.

There are a few excellent electronically controlled brooders on the market, and if the owner is fortunate enough to be able to purchase one of these, temperature regulation becomes much simpler. However, the chick will still need close observation to ensure that the temperature settings are comfortable and appropriate.

A brooder cover will be needed. This can be a terry bath towel or something fancier. My mother and I knitted several pastel-colored covers, which add a pretty touch to the nursery furnishings. The purpose of a brooder cover is twofold. First, it serves to keep the heat in, as glass radiates heat into the atmosphere very rapidly. Second, it provides the privacy the young chick needs in order to rest and sleep. During the day, one end of the cover can be lifted so the chick can see out and become accustomed to normal household activity. As the chick grows, remaining awake longer, as well as needing less external heat, the cover can be lifted from the sides and front of the brooder for much of the day, being replaced only at night when the chick's activity level prepares it for sleep.

The brooder must be cleaned and disinfected thoroughly at least once a week. For young chicks, the bedding should be changed at least every two days. For larger chicks whose droppings have begun to approach the volume of an adult bird's, bedding should be changed every day. When disinfecting, it is important to remember that no disinfectant will work until the surfaces are thoroughly cleaned of droppings, food particles, damp bedding, etc. Only after the brooder is completely washed with hot soapy water and is squeaky clean should disinfectant be applied. The *wet* disinfectant should remain on all surfaces *at least ten minutes*. The brooder must then be thoroughly rinsed and dried to prevent any possible toxic reaction. Appropriate disinfectants include bleach, Lysol™, and Wavecide™—all diluted to the manufacturer's recommendations. For an in-depth discussion of disinfectants, see *The Parrot in Health and Illness*.

In addition to the basics of container, heat source, and hygiene, the brooder should contain one or two safe, colorful toys. Human baby rattles, such as those with large, colorful keys are a good choice. Sturdy bells are also suitable. The rule of thumb is that no parts should be toxic or easily detached by the chick. They should lend themselves to easy cleaning, also. I find that the easiest way to attach the toys to the inside of the brooder is with the use of suction cups equipped with hooks, such as the kind used to hang stained glass ornaments on windows. These should be placed on the *outside* of the brooder, and the toy attachment threaded up over the edge of the brooder and hooked onto the suction cup. This will cause the brooder cover to sit slightly ajar, but this is usually no problem. A thin coat of petroleum jelly around the edge of the suction cup will ensure that it does not fall off, dumping both toy and cup into the brooder, where the chick might injure itself on them. When the chick is strong enough to jerk the toys off, they should be removed and replaced with playthings more appropriate to its size and increasing strength.

Another important item for the brooder is a small, cuddly toy. It should be placed in the back corner of the brooder, where most chicks prefer to sleep. This provides a sense of security for the chick and something soft to cuddle when it sleeps. Again, the cuddly toy should have no moving parts, or anything—such as buttons for eyes—the chick can remove and swallow.

The last item older chicks enjoy are the chiming bathtub toys made for human toddlers. The smallest ones made are suitable for parrot chicks. Some are clear, with colorful inserts that spin when the ball is pushed. When chicks are old enough to manipulate these around the brooder, they provide fun and exercise, helping to teach the chick to amuse itself.

Next on our agenda is *the chick's need for rest*. This is especially important in the early Transitional Stage, when the downy chick has only a few pin feathers poking through here and there. Its needs now primarily concern nutrition, growth, and rest. In this respect, the chick's needs are like those of a human infant. Because all the chick's metabolic energy will be spent eating, digesting, and growing, it needs a *lot* of rest and sleep. Moving about and playing are not in the energy budget at this point. Therefore, respect the young parrot's need for adequate rest. The brooder should be kept dim to facilitate rest and sleep. The small, cuddly toy in the back corner will really pay dividends during this time, in terms of providing extra softness and comforting warmth to the chick.

Respect the chick's very real need for uninterrupted rest and sleep, and don't disturb it. As feeding time approaches, the chick will awaken, become restless, and will usually begin peeping most pitifully, just in case you might have

Doane

Gabriel, the author's eleven-week-old Timneh African Grey, enjoys playing on his back with his toys. He is holding a small stuffed dinosaur.

forgotten its hungry tummy! At this time, it is fine to pick it up for some gentle cuddling and kissing before preparing its formula. Just be sure it is not out of the brooder long enough to become chilled. And be sure not to kiss it on the beak or face—human germs can cause problems for small chicks, whose immune systems are not yet fully functional. Once the chick has been fed, don't play with it or handle it other than to replace it comfortably in the brooder. Excessive handling may cause the baby to "burp" up contents of the full crop and possibly aspirate some food into its lungs.

As the chick matures and progresses to the late phase of the Transitional Stage, it will have a fairly full coat of contour feathers and be much better able to regulate its own body temperature. It will also spend much more time awake between feedings. It is now a good idea to keep the cover partially off the sides of the brooder, so the baby can observe and become comfortable with the home it will occupy when it achieves "big bird" status. During the waking periods, gently playing and talking with it is appropriate. Be careful not to overdo it, though, or a very spoiled youngster will result. The chick should be learning, even this early, to amuse itself with its toys and by watching household activities.

Nutrition for the Transitional Chick

Probably more chicks die from feeding-related problems than from any other cause. This is because new owners are rarely given the proper information and background on this all-important aspect of rearing a chick. At best, they may have given one or two supervised feedings to the baby before taking it home. Because the actual mechanics of getting the food into the chick are relatively simple, albeit messy the first few times, owners often mistakenly believe that hand-feeding a young parrot is "a piece of cake." It can be—if nothing goes wrong. Unfortunately, there are many things that can go wrong and often do. This is very sad for the owner and often tragic for the chick.

Owners of unweaned chicks need to know all the following in order to rear them to fledging uneventfully:

- How to select an appropriate, safe nestling formula.

- How to store formula safely.

- How to prepare formula safely.

- How to choose safe, appropriate feeding implements and disinfect them thoroughly.

- Effective hygiene for owner and chick.

- How to get the maximum amount of formula inside the chick, rather than everywhere else.

- How many times per day to feed the chick, and how much to feed it each time.

- How to gauge a chick's progress.

- How to know when things may be going wrong in time to correct them.

This may seem like a lot to learn, and the reader may question whether it is all necessary. It is. Don't be like one gentleman who said to me, "Oh, this is just more stupid stuff I really don't need to know." He later came to regret his cavalier attitude. His parrot also regretted it.

Let's take one item at a time. You will find that "all of this stuff" isn't really so very much after all, as it all dovetails very neatly in actual practice.

How to select an appropriate, safe nestling formula: There are many good prepared formulas on the market. Some companies now prepare formula specific to certain kinds of parrots. It is now known that macaw nestlings require higher fat content in their diets than do other parrot species. In addition, nestling macaws seem to be prone to mineralization of the kidneys, a condition that is often incompatible with life. I highly recommend, then, that formula products specifically produced for nestling macaws be used if you are hand-feeding one of these magnificent birds. The following excellent companies make these products:

- KayTee™: 1-800-669-9580

- Pretty Bird™: 1-800-356-5020

- Roudybush™: 1-800-326-1726

They also make nestling formulas for other parrot species.

Do not be tempted to make your own formula. There are still a few breeders using the old formula recipes, which usually call for monkey chow. Monkey chow often contains the infamous bacteria E. coli, which is extremely harmful to all parrots and can be devastating in the unweaned chick. Additionally, homemade formulas are always unbalanced or completely lacking in essential nutrients, vitamins, and minerals. This can lead to many problems, including rickets and malformed beaks.

Do not add vitamins, minerals, or any other supplementation of these types to commercial formulas. These are balanced for the nestling, and further additions can cause real harm.

How to store formula safely: All commercial formula products are dry and must be reconstituted before use. The dry, unreconstituted formula must be refrigerated or, better yet, frozen. They must never be kept on a kitchen counter or in a cupboard. This allows harmful bacteria to contaminate the formula material, causing illness in the chick.

How to prepare formula safely: In general, the formula should be as thick as the chick can handle from the feeding implement. A good consistency to aim for is that of thick split pea soup. It should be served at a temperature of 104 to 108 degrees Fahrenheit. Do not gauge the temperature by sprinkling it on your wrist or dipping a finger into it. *A cooking thermometer must be used.* Some chicks prefer their formula at the higher end of the range, others on the cooler end. If the chick seems to be reluctant to take the feeding, offer it warmer or cooler, as required, but it should always be within the recommended 104-to-108-degree range.

Formula must always be prepared fresh for each feeding. Once the formula has been reconstituted, it becomes a potent medium for bacterial growth if allowed to sit, even in the refrigerator. It is foolish economy to prepare a day's batch for the sake of convenience, only to have a chick sicken. In this case, the best scenario is a costly vet bill resulting in a surviving chick. In the worst case, the chick will die and you will still have a costly vet bill. Don't economize on a few cents worth of formula and a few extra minutes of your time!

The first step in formula preparation is to place the needed amount of water in a small container. It is preferable to use water that has been boiled and kept in the refrigerator. Distilled water or nursery water can also be used, but it is not sterile. A new portion of boiled water should be prepared every twenty-four hours. The dried formula mix is added *after* the water is heated. Follow the manufacturer's directions about ratio of water to dried mix. If you find it too thin or too thick, you can experiment until it is the right consistency.

Heat the needed amount of water in a microwave oven until it is hot. The amount of time needed will vary from unit to unit, so again, you will have to experiment. After the water is heated, add the dried formula in the amount needed to produce the required consistency. *Stir thoroughly* to avoid hot spots that can burn the baby's crop. A burned crop can cause death; at best, surgery will be required to repair the damage. After the formula has been stirred well, test in several spots with a thermometer to be sure it is at the right temperature for feeding.

How to choose safe, appropriate feeding implements and disinfect them thoroughly: The "weapon of choice" for feeding your chick is largely a matter of owner preference. Some use feeding syringes or pipettes; others use spoons. *Never* use a feeding needle. This is a stainless steel tube that fits onto the hub of a syringe. The needle is inserted into the chick's mouth, down its throat, and into its crop. The crop is then filled quickly and at one time with one push of the syringe, which holds a predetermined amount of formula. This feeding method is entirely unnecessary, dangerous in unskilled hands, and often results in weaning problems because the youngster has never really tasted food and must actually be taught what food is. The only justification for the use of a feeding needle is as an emergency measure to provide food for a sick bird that will not otherwise eat. This should be done only by a qualified professional.

Feeding syringes, unlike feeding needles, are inserted into the baby's mouth, at the side of the beak, and formula is gently pushed into its mouth when the baby begins to pump its head in the feeding response. A feeding pipette is very similar in its use. Both have the advantage of quick food delivery with little mess— if you're skilled and lucky! Because syringes are marked in CCs, and pipettes come in various predetermined CC measurements, it is easy to know how much food the baby has taken. The disadvantage is that it is sometimes difficult to gauge how quickly the baby can swallow formula, and it is possible to choke it if the formula goes in too fast.

A stainless steel spoon makes an excellent feeding implement and is my choice for feeding babies. The sides of the spoon must be bent upward at an approximate 30-degree angle in order to contain the formula efficiently. Although the spoon is not marked in CCs, it is still easy to tell how much food the baby has eaten by keeping count of the number of spoonfuls used. A baby spoon, used with very young chicks or those of small species, holds two CCs. A teaspoon holds five CCs. A tablespoon, good for use with very large chicks, holds fifteen CCs. The advantages of the spoon include ease of use and a far smaller chance of aspirating the baby, because it can take the formula from the spoon at its own rate. An additional benefit is that formula can be made thicker if required as the chick matures. Very thick formula will not pass through a feeding syringe with ease.

It is extremely important that feeding implements, regardless of the type used, be first thoroughly cleaned, then stored in a disinfectant solution between uses. If syringes are being used, it will be necessary to replace them every two or three days, as disinfectants will soon destroy the rubber cap at the end of the syringe's plunger. An excellent disinfectant for use with feeding tools is Wavecide™. At this writing, it is one of the few disinfectants available to the hand-feeder that will kill—without exception—all known bacteria, viruses, and fungi and is the only one I recommend. This product can be ordered from most avian supply houses. Your veterinarian can also order it for you, and some pet stores carry it. Place the disinfectant in a glass container, diluted to manufacturer's directions. After cleaning, feeding implements are stored in this container between feedings. Before using feeding implements, all disinfectant must be carefully rinsed off; otherwise, the baby will ingest the solution and become ill.

Feeding containers should be put through the dishwasher with heated water and sani-rinse.

Effective feeding hygiene for owner and chick: Unweaned parrot babies have immature immune systems. This means that they don't have the resistance to fight off infections very well, so it is absolutely essential that they be protected from potential germ problems. Before preparing formula, the owner must wash his or her hands thoroughly using an antibacterial liquid soap. There are several brands available at most supermarkets, packaged in pump dispensers. Refills are also commonly available. Bar soap, believe it or not, can grow bacteria very well indeed; therefore, the recommendation is to use a dispenser. Use paper towels for drying, as they are more sanitary. And be sure your hands remain warm after washing, especially if you will be handling a young chick without much down or many feathers. Imagine what it would be like to be scooped up for your feeding by cold, clammy hands! It might just rob you of your appetite.

After the chick has been fed, clean any dribbled formula from skin and feathers using a soft paper towel moistened with warm water. If necessary, pat the baby dry before putting it back in the brooder. Be sure no formula dries and crusts around the chick's beak or under its tongue. It may occasionally be necessary to wipe out formula retained under the tongue with a sterile cotton swab. Be sure to inspect feet and toenails: Baby parrots walk about in their droppings. If this is allowed to cake on feet and around nails, bacterial problems and resulting nail bed deformities can occur.

If you are hand-feeding two or more chicks, each should have its own container of formula and its own feeding implement.

Anytime the chick is to be handled, whether for feeding, cuddling, or any other reason, the owner should wash his or her hands—no exceptions.

How to get the maximum amount of formula inside the chick, rather than everywhere else: Once you get the hang of it, this will not be a problem. The first thing to start with is a hungry chick. Chicks usually *are* hungry at feeding time. But there are exceptions, mostly when the baby has progressed to the point at which it requires fewer feedings per day. Occasionally, the chick may still be a little sleepy, or its attention may be caught by something in its surroundings, or you may have a chick that is a lazy eater. (The chick that is normally an eager eater, then suddenly loses interest for two or more feedings, should be seen by the veterinarian.)

When feeding your chick, place it on an easily grasped surface, such as a folded bath towel on the kitchen counter. By refolding the towel, you can get two to four uses before consigning it to the laundry.

Parrot babies ingest formula by pumping their heads up and down vigorously while eating. This is the same response they used when being fed by their natural /mothers. Most chicks will start to bob their heads as soon as they see food approaching. If this is the case, place the syringe or pipette at the side of the beak towards the back, and begin delivering formula slowly and smoothly.

A change of formula may be in order for the older chick that is tired of the usual offering.

Alternate beak sides from one feeding to the next to avoid causing beak deformities. If you use a spoon, place the tip inside the chick's mouth at the front and angle so the formula slides off easily into the chick's mouth. As the crop fills, the pumping will become less enthusiastic and taper off. Some chicks will continue to beg after the crop is full. Such chicks must not be given additional formula.

**The crop is a food storage organ that rests at the
top of the chick's breastbone.**

If, however, the chick seems more interested in everything else but eating, try lightly massaging the soft pads at the beak's edges. These are located at the back, where upper and lower beak come together. This usually will elicit a feeding response, and then you're on your way! Dribbling a little warm formula into the chick's mouth will also usually start the baby.

Sometimes as chicks grow, they develop an aversion to the hand-feeding formula currently being used. If this should happen, try switching to another comparable brand with similar nutrient content. Some breeders have noted that as certain chicks mature, they not only have a better developed sense of taste, but more tongue control. A change of taste or texture may be just the thing your growing nestling needs if it begins to wrinkle up its little beak when you approach with the same old ho-hum formula.

How many times per day to feed the chick, and how much to feed each time: Generally speaking, the chick in the early phase of the Transitional Stage will need four feedings per day. These should come at 6 to 7 A.M., noon, 4 to 5 P.M., and 9 to 10 P.M. Within reason, depending on the chick's needs and preferences, you can adjust the times to allow for a bit of convenience for yourself. But a chick should never be allowed to cry with an empty crop for extended periods. It is not good for its physical or emotional health.

The chick in the late phase of the Transitional Stage will need three feedings per day. Judging when to eliminate a feeding is something of an art. Clues about this are good feather coat; actually eating offered weaning foods, rather than

Cole

Four-week-old Blue-fronted Amazons with properly filled crops.

nibbling or playing with them; partially full crop at the noon feeding; dramatically decreased formula intake at noon feeding; and complete lack of interest in noon feeding. If most or all of this is happening regularly, eliminate the noon feeding and offer a 2 P.M. feeding. The feeding schedule would then be 6 to 7 A.M., 2 P.M., and 9 to 10 P.M.

It is very important to know when enough is enough when feeding your chick. *The crop must not be overfilled.* The crop is the food storage organ. It rests at the top of the chick's breastbone (see drawing). As the chick takes formula, the crop can be seen to fill. Usually, the chick's feeding response will taper off as the crop fills and the baby experiences a sense of satiety. Now, gently feel the crop with your index finger. If it still feels like a half-filled water balloon, continue feeding until the crop fills, but has a nice "give." When this occurs, stop the feeding. If the crop has the feeling and appearance of being literally as tight as a drum, the baby has been given too much formula. If this happens once in a while, no great harm is done, although be careful when putting the baby in the brooder not to place any pressure on the overfull crop. However, if consistent over-filling is occurring, crop tone will be lost, leading to difficulty emptying. This predisposes the baby to the real possibility of infection because food is being retained too long, providing an excellent environment for fungal and bacterial growth.

How to gauge a chick's progress: The baby should show daily weight gains (except during the weaning process, when it will actually begin to lose some weight). It should be acquiring an ever-increasing covering of body (contour)

Cole

These six-week-old Orange-winged Amazon chicks have been fed just the right amount. Their crops are full, but not distended.

feathers. Its eyes should be bright, and it should be awake for increasing periods of time between feedings. This time should be spent preening, playing, observing its surroundings with interest, practicing motor skills such as walking and balancing on one foot; experimenting with and gradually eating more weaning foods, and making comfort movements like wing stretching. The droppings should begin to show a difference in consistency as a result of ingested weaning foods.

However, the best gauge of the maturing nestling's health is still the weight chart. Be sure to keep track daily of weight, number of feedings, and amount taken at each feeding, as well as comments about developmental landmarks reached and anything else noteworthy that you want to remember. Use the weight and weaning charts in this chapter as guidelines. If your bird's species is not mentioned, weights and weaning times for similar species can be used as a rough guideline. Breeders usually keep records that may help you determine whether your baby is on schedule or lagging seriously.

How to know when things are going wrong in time to correct them: As you work daily with your chick, you will begin to develop a real feel for what this small creature is all about. You will reach the point where you can anticipate its moods and know almost instinctively what's going on with it. You will develop a "sixth sense" about when things are right—or wrong. Never ignore your feelings about things being "not quite right." I have a very good breeder friend whose motto is "When you think something's wrong, it probably is." Although this may sound a bit pessimistic, it is this kind of careful attention that can save a parrot's life. Early intervention in health problems is the key to preserving your bird's well-being.

Pay careful attention to anything that gives rise to concern. Although I have already listed the major danger signals, it is worth repeating them.

- Failure to gain weight, or actual weight loss, unless the chick has entered the weaning phase.

- A crop that fails to empty completely between feedings, especially if it remains partially full overnight (unless the chick is in the weaning phase).

- A crop that feels doughy when empty and rolled between thumb and index fingers.

- A baby that has lost its normal pink color and/or feels cool to the touch.

- Lack of feeding response when the crop is empty and it is feeding time (unless the chick is in the weaning phase).

- Continual whining and restlessness.

- Beak deformities or splayed legs.

- Change in quality or consistency of droppings (unless the chick is in the weaning phase and is eating a lot of weaning foods rather than formula).

Any of the above warrant a call to your avian veterinarian. He or she may be able to advise over the telephone or may want to see the chick at the office. Be sure to keep the chick warm while awaiting the veterinarian's advice. Extra humidity should be supplied by placing a tightly covered container of warm water in the brooder. It should have a broad base so it cannot be easily upset. The water should not be so hot that the chick will burn itself if it touches the container. Holes punched in the container lid will allow the moisture to permeate the brooder while protecting the chick from accidental drowning. If the chick is large enough to capsize a container of water, you can place the brooder in a small warm room such as a bathroom and run a steam vaporizer. Do not aim the steam nozzle directly at the brooder.

Ailing chicks need to be kept well hydrated. Ordinarily, they obtain adequate water from the formula mixture. If the chick refuses formula, a feeding of warm Gatorade™ or Pedialyte™ should be attempted. Another good product for use in this situation is Hagen's Day One™ (1-888-BY HAGEN). It is specially formulated for use with young chicks, although it can also be used with adult parrots needing hydration. The Hagen number given above will also allow the caller to access the company's technical support service.

Products such as those mentioned are preferable to plain water because they contain calories and electrolytes. When using such products, remember that they should be given warm, just as with formula.

Environmental Enrichment

Given a healthy, well-nourished baby whose physical needs are being met, enrichment is the single most important element in rearing a well-adjusted parrot able to take its place as a "civilized" member of the family. The purposes of enrichment are fourfold. First, it provides stimulation the growing nestling needs for its great intelligence. Second, it starts the parrot at an early age on the road to learning how to amuse itself and enjoy its own company. Third, it helps develop

**Parrots instinctively fear overhead move-
ment unless taught otherwise.**

a bird accustomed to new and different things, thus equipping it to cope with new objects, people, and circumstances in its life without crippling fear. Fourth, it's just plain fun for parrot and owner alike.

The advantage of allowing the chick unobstructed views from the brooder into the room as it grows older and is awake for periods of time has already been discussed. Also covered was the use of appropriate, safe brooder toys. There are other things, however, that will add visual and auditory richness to the growing nestling's life.

Crib mobiles are not only visually attractive to parrot babies, but have music boxes they love to listen to. Hanging one of these close to the brooder where the baby can see and hear it at various times during the day will provide a colorful, fascinating focal point for the chick. It will also accustom it to an object moving overhead and thereby diminish the usual instinctive fear parrots have of unfamiliar objects. This will pay dividends in the future, as the chick will be much more amenable to hands moving over its head to pet or scratch it. This can be difficult for many parrots to accept if they have not been helped to learn that hands are friendly, not fatal.

Use of music is also extremely desirable in the chick's enrichment program. An audiocassette player can usually be placed close to the brooder and used to play nursery songs, lullabies, soft classical music, or environmental tapes. Care should be taken that musical and environmental selections used are not brash and loud. Later in life, your parrot may thoroughly enjoy your favorite rock group or a recording of a summer thunderstorm. However, these are frightening for the nestling.

For the youngster that is about to graduate to a weaning cage or has already done so, read aloud to your chick perched on your arm. Don't laugh! Not only is this enjoyable for the owner—I have become reacquainted over the years with all my childhood favorites, and find I enjoy them as much now as I did as a child—but it is also very enjoyable for the parrot chick. It provides a short structured time every day or so in which the chick has your undivided attention—a great way to cement the bonding process. It

Reading aloud to your parrot is a great means of bonding.

also provides the chick with the experience of cadence and intonation of human speech, which may in time allow it to learn to talk more easily. In addition, reading to your chick will help develop its attention span. It is a great way to introduce the chick to the experience of being "in the great, wide world" in a positive, secure, predictable setting.

Nursery rhymes and very short stories with lots of colorful pictures are good choices for the parrot youngster embarking on its literary voyage. Use lots of expression. As you read, point out the pictures and talk to the chick about them. If your family laughs, let them! You'll be the one having all the fun. If you find this activity is one both of

Most parrots enjoy being sung to.

you continue to enjoy, as the parrot becomes older and develops a longer attention span, you can progress to longer stories.

Last, if you like to sing and have a pleasant voice, sing to your chick. Chicks adore it! (I believe I did give fair warning that rearing a parrot is very much like rearing a human infant.)

The Weaning Stage (Locomotory Stage)

When your parrot chick reaches this stage, it is well on its way to becoming grown up, at least in terms of physical development. It will still have a way to go before being completely socialized and trained. By now, it may have outgrown the brooder and have an almost full coat of feathers, although the flight and tail feathers will not be completely grown. A move to the weaning cage may be indicated, which will be discussed further on. It will also have been introduced to weaning foods several weeks ago and may be eating these supplemental foods well. However, it may still be merely nibbling and playing with your offerings. Each chick is slightly different in its weaning pattern.

This period, when the chick is perfecting its physical skills and learning to self-feed, is very energy-consuming, as well as being psychologically stressful. The transition from dependence to independence does not occur in one smooth curve, but in starts and stops, regression, then leaps of progress. It cannot be rushed, and owners must use great patience when shepherding their young bird through this period.

There are three primary things with which the owner must be concerned when his or her chick reaches the Locomotory Stage:

Doane

- One, helping the chick to become entirely self-feeding, safely and comfortably.

- Two, providing appropriate housing for the parrot.

This eight-and-a-half-week-old Green-cheeked Amazon is well on its way through the Locomotory Stage.

- Three, beginning the first formal training period.

Weaning a parrot is an art. A program cannot be set down in black and white and followed rigidly. Fortunately, parrot chicks are genetically programmed with a drive toward independence. So no matter how slow the process, the owner can be assured his or her chick will wean, no matter how it dawdles through the process— unless the owner is unwittingly prolonging it for some reason. This is the silver lining to the cloud that proclaims in exasper-

Parrot chicks do eventually wean, even though it sometimes seems they never will!

ated and mournful tones, "This bird should be weaned by now. Am I going to have to hand-feed it 'til it's twenty-five?"

One of the most harmful things owners can do at this time is to force the nestling to wean completely before it is ready. In addition to the emotional damage, the parrot's physical health will suffer, because it will be deprived of necessary nutrients. It may also become dehydrated, because it has not yet learned to

**During the first part of the Locomotory Stage,
parrot chicks weigh more than their parents.**

drink water. It is better to err on the side of leniency in weaning than to try forcing the issue. Occasionally a bird refuses to wean, a problem that will be discussed further on. However, the vast majority wean more or less on schedule.

Before continuing, *pre-weaning peak weight* must be considered. Chicks in the nest or brooder mainly sleep and grow. All parrot chicks at some point weigh more than their parents! It can be a soft life, but alas, all good things come to an end, and the parrot chick, like it or not, must prepare for its first flight and independence. Since it is difficult to fly when you're overweight, owing to a tremendous wing-load problem, the only solution is to slim down. And this is just what Mother Nature does for the chick. By the time it's ready for the first solo flight, it may have lost as much as 15 to 20 percent of its body weight. The same thing happens with the chick in the brooder. It begins to eat a bit on its own. Its crop shrinks to adult size. It becomes more active. *Voilà!* The plump baby is now the avian equivalent of an Olympic athlete.

In light of this, the owner should be prepared to see a weight loss in the chick right around the end of the Transitional Stage or the beginning of the Locomotory Stage. Consult the charts to assure yourself that your chick's weight loss is within the normal limits. If it is excessive, or you're concerned that something may be wrong, then a call to the vet is in order. But this moderate weight loss in the direction of adult weight is perfectly normal and nothing to be concerned about when the chick seems well and healthy in all other respects. The loss will level out when the youngster has been completely self-feeding for a week or so. It may even gain a bit of weight, which is fine.

Food

By the time the nestling has reached the Locomotory Stage, it should have been supplied with weaning foods for several weeks prior. The owner should have been keeping an eye out for the signs of weaning food interest in the Transitional Stage. If not, *now* is the time to start offering these goodies. They should be available at all times during the day, along with fresh water. You may have to change the water several times a day, because parrot chicks love dunking a variety of things in it, then wandering off and leaving them there to create "stew." Moist foods such as minced vegetables and fruits should be replaced two or three times a day, especially in warm weather.

Place weaning food and fresh water in small, tip-proof glazed ceramic crocks in an easily accessible place on the cage bottom until the young bird learns to perch efficiently. Use only glazed ceramic manufactured in the United States, since foreign products may use glaze containing lead. Do not put the bowls where the chick usually deposits droppings. After the chick is perching well and is comfortable with this, conventional parrot bowls can be secured to the cage side at the end of the perch.

At the beginning of the Locomotory Stage, the chick may still be taking three feedings a day, in the early morning, mid-afternoon, and before bedtime. The usual weaning pattern is for the chick to begin losing interest in the afternoon feeding. This occurs when the chick is eating weaning foods well enough to satisfy hunger pangs during the day. When this takes place, withdraw this feeding, but retain the early morning and late evening feedings. Continue to monitor the chick's weight daily, first thing in the morning. Also check the quantity and quality of the droppings. They should be more formed as a result of solid food intake. There should be a reasonable amount of green or brownish-tan feces in proportion to urates and liquid urine. If you are seeing only urates and urine with little fecal material, an extra feeding is in order. The chick may see-saw back and forth like this for several days before routinely and comfortably doing without the afternoon feeding.

As the chick matures, it will begin to lose interest in the morning feeding. At this point, only the before-bedtime feeding will be retained. Continue to monitor weight and droppings. It may be several weeks before the chick is ready to give up the evening feeding, even if it is eating plenty on its own. In this respect, the chick is rather like the toddler that still needs a bedtime bottle for security. Eventually, the chick will give up this feeding, also.

At this point, the owner may want to try a little gentle experimentation, especially if the parrot is suspected of a bit of sneaky manipulation and emotional blackmail. If the chick is maintaining its weight, its droppings are satisfactory, and its crop still has some food in it at bedtime, spend a few minutes with it, then simply cover the cage and put birdie to bed. A few pathetic wails may be voiced, but if they are rather half-hearted and die away as the chick goes to sleep, you can safely ignore them. Weigh the chick the next morning. If no significant weight loss has occurred and it attacks its morning rations with gusto, you are justified in concluding it has withstood, without problems, the horror of no bedtime feeding.

Repeat the procedure the next night. If all goes well and the chick remains robust, playful, and in good appetite, congratulations! Your chick is to all intents and purposes weaned. And don't for a minute let it sucker you into feeding it again. Parrots can be clever little devils.

Problems of the Nonweaning Parrot

Roughly speaking, the parrot that refuses to wean more than a month past the expected time frame has a problem. It may be the parrot's problem, or it may be the owner's.

Problems originating with the bird include mild bacterial infections and/or gut yeast infections. Take the bird to your avian vet and insist on crop and vent cultures. These problems are easily resolved with medication, and in most cases, the result is an almost miraculous change in the chick's attitude toward self-feeding.

Sometimes owners unwittingly prolong the process. They may enjoy caring for a dependent baby and are reluctant to give this up. Some may feel insecure about the weaning process and fear harming the baby. Others may have waited too late to introduce weaning food, missing the optimum time for the chick to experiment with "real" food and prolonging the process. And in yet other cases, the owner may not understand the weaning process and therefore may be unable to facilitate it.

Obviously if your parrot refuses to wean, you must look at both the bird and yourself to determine both cause and remedy. There is no such thing as a parrot that will never wean, so take heart and go forward confidently. You, too, will one day be the owner of a completely weaned parrot!

Housing

The next issue is the *appropriate housing* for the weaning parrot youngster. The cage should be placed in its permanent position in the house before the chick is transferred. It may be helpful to do this several days before the move is to be made, taking the chick two or three times a day to see its new "house" so it becomes familiar with this strange-looking contraption, as well as the room in which it has been placed. The chick can even be placed inside the cage for a few minutes, under your supervision, provided the perch and other furnishings have been appropriately modified—a subject to be discussed soon. Remember to speak softly and reassuringly to the youngster, explaining what the cage is and how much it will enjoy the "privileges of being a big bird."

In most cases, the weaning cage will be the parrot's permanent home. Therefore, some modifications will need to be made for the new, young occupant, as cages are nearly always designed for adult parrots. Young parrots are very clumsy; often, they will not yet be able to perch efficiently when moved to the weaning cage. The placement of perches and food bowls will need to be altered. Additionally, the grates supplied with most cages have the wires arranged too far apart to accommodate the young parrot's feet.

The cage grate should be covered with a thick towel, folded if necessary. You may want to remove the grate altogether until your youngster has learned to perch with confidence and prefers the perch to the cage floor. If the cage grate has been removed, it is still better to use soft toweling, rather than newspapers, as this will give the chick more secure footing. Because the towel will become quickly soiled with food and droppings, it must be replaced at least once a day and laundered. Two towels, one for wash and one for wear, make things much simpler.

Food and water bowls must be tip-proof, glazed ceramic, and placed in cage corners away from the area the chick uses to relieve itself. One each for dry food, wet food, and water are recommended. Water and wet food must be changed as necessary to prevent spoilage and contamination.

Placement of the perch is very important. Initially, it should be only two or three inches from the cage bottom (or grate, if it has been retained). However, care must be taken to position it to prevent the chick from sticking its head underneath and becoming pinned there. When the chick becomes proficient at perching and is climbing well, the perch can be placed at standard height. At this time, food bowls can be positioned at the perch ends, on the cage sides. At first, leave bowls on the cage bottom, also. It may take a day or two for the chick to discover food is available at perch height.

It is interesting to note that some youngsters showing reluctance to wean may "see the light" once food and water bowls are placed above the cage floor. Whether this is due to an inborn aversion to bottom feeding, or whether it is just an individual preference, is hard to say.

Two or three safe, age-appropriate toys may be placed in the cage in positions that allow the parrot easy access. Save swing perches for the youngster that is absolutely confident in perching and climbing ability.

The continued use of a cage cover is highly recommended. It provides security and decreases stimuli from the room outside when the youngster is ready to sleep at night. All parrots should have a regular bedtime as part of their daily routine. Cage covers facilitate this, while at the same time allowing family members to use the room past Polly's bedtime.

When the day arrives for the big move, don't forget to move its cuddly toy to the cage. Doing this provides something familiar and comforting in the midst of such a big change. Many chicks will prefer to sleep on the cage floor with their "granny" for some time after moving in. This is another reason why soft, cloth toweling is recommended on the floor or grate of the cage. Depending upon your chick's reaction, or if nights are very cold, it is certainly permissible to return it to the brooder at night for the first five to seven days. Doing this allows for a good night's rest if the bird seems overwhelmed by the transition to the weaning cage, or if you worry about cold night temperatures. It is not recommended that a heating pad be affixed to the side of the cage. The danger of the youngster gnawing it and electrocuting itself is too great.

Continued Socialization and Training

First, just because the parrot is now in a conventional cage, do not stop your enrichment program. Indeed, all parrots need this kind of sensory enrichment throughout their lives. They are intelligent, curious creatures and thrive on the novelty of new music, television, being read and sung to, and other expressions of "togetherness."

Soucek

Gizmo, Gayle Soucek's Timneh African Grey, will take his teddy bear with him when he moves to a weaning cage.

Second, all through the pre-weaning cage period, the owner should have been using the "Up" command when removing the baby from the brooder for any reason. Having done this will greatly facilitate the chick's progress when formal lessons in the Basic Three commence.

Third, during this early time in the weaning cage, the youngster must learn immediately that it is to come out whenever the owner wishes. Some chicks, especially at first, tend to cower in the corner and are most reluctant to come out, because everything is so new and slightly frightening. When this occurs, merely lift the chick out as you have been doing when the brooder was in use, being sure to use the "Up" command. Be firm and gentle, but do it. Don't allow yourself to "cut any slack" for the chick. By doing so, you teach it that it can call the shots, planting the seeds for territoriality and "cage-boundness." You are also inadvertently teaching the chick to be afraid of any area outside the cage.

Many chicks will still be on a twice-daily feeding schedule, in addition to eating weaning foods. At this point, the dry offerings should gradually be replaced with the parrot pellet of your choice. Continue to offer fresh fruits, vegetables, and thawed frozen corn—either minced or in larger pieces, depending on the chick's current preference.

When the chick is perching confidently and has adjusted to the new housing, you may begin the first formal training sessions, starting with the first of the Three Basic Obedience Skills explained in detail in chapter 5. The program should be followed just as faithfully as for a weaned youngster just brought home. The fact that you have partially reared, then weaned the bird makes no difference in the parrot's need to learn these very necessary behaviors.

Last, do allow the parrot time in its cage to play, to learn to enjoy its own company, and thereby to learn it is not the center of the universe. Many future potential problems are avoided in this way.

A final note on the youngster in the weaning cage: At some point, usually unexpectedly, the chick will lift off and fly for the first time. It has fledged! Let its first flight be its last, for all the reasons previously discussed. Make an appointment with the avian vet for its first wing feather trim. As time goes on, you'll have good reason to be glad you did, especially when you begin to hear the many horror stories about dear pets that flew into the wild blue yonder and were never able to find their way home.

What Has Been Learned in This Chapter?

- Many people buy unweaned parrots believing this will facilitate the human/parrot bond; this is not always true.

- The primary goal in rearing an unweaned parrot is to keep it alive and healthy so it will successfully wean and go on to effective training and socialization.

- Training and socialization of the unweaned parrot actually begins as soon as the nestling comes to its new home, although it is subtle, informal, and completely noninvasive.

- The owner of an unweaned parrot must have the necessary equipment and knowledge to rear his or her chick without serious problems.

- A daily, complete record of the chick's food intake, weight, and other pertinent information must be kept.

- The owner must know what is normal for a chick of the species he or she is rearing.

- All unweaned chicks have the same basic needs: adequate rest and sleep, good nutrition, proper ambient temperature, environmental enrichment, and confident, gentle handling by the owner.

- Owners of unweaned chicks must recognize the warning signs of impending health problems and be prepared to consult the avian vet if these signs appear.

- Most unweaned chicks are acquired in the Transitional or Locomotory Stages, and the chick's needs will change as it matures and passes from one stage to the next.

- Weaning is physically and emotionally stressful for the chick, and the owner must use knowledge and patience to help it successfully complete this process.

- A newly weaned chick is not an adult, even though it may physically appear to be one.

- Enrichment must continue throughout the parrot's life and must not stop when the chick moves to a weaning cage.

- The "Up" command must be used consistently throughout the rearing period.

- It is absolutely essential that the parrot reared by the owner go through the formal training program of the Three Basic Obedience Skills, just as any other parrot. *Hand-rearing the parrot does not render this training unnecessary.*

8

Potty Training

> *To every thing there is a season, and a*
> *time to every purpose under heaven.*

> —Ecclesiastes 3:1

Dealing with pet wastes exists whether we have dogs, cats, furry little mammals, or birds. Dog owners are leashed to pooper scoopers and late-night walks in all weather—or cleaning up the backyard with wearisome regularity. Cat owners must deal with litter pans, cleaning them daily, often as their feline companions watch laconically for the first opportunity to jump into the freshly cleaned pan.

However, cat and dog owners have an advantage over bird owners with respect to their pets' potty habits in that there is a designated place for elimination to occur. Parrots generally let nature take its course wherever they happen to be. This presents a real problem for those of us who often have our parrots out and about the house with us.

But need it be a problem?

Not always, especially with the larger parrots. These birds can be toilet trained to a certain extent, some more successfully than others. Some parrots, like Miss Molly, my Umbrella Cockatoo, train themselves. Molly has an inborn aversion to depositing her droppings on humans, which is fortunate for us. Not once in all the years she has shared her life with us has she ever left a mess on a shoulder or lap.

There are also devices that can be fitted over the toilet bowl, complete with wire grate to prevent the bird from falling in. They allow the parrot to perch over the bowl and deposit its droppings. Creative Bird Accessories markets such a potty perch (1-800-765-2325; or e-mail to CREATBIRD@aol.com). Needless to say, even with such a helpful piece of equipment, the parrot should never be left sitting in the bathroom unsupervised.

There is no doubt about it: Having a parrot that is trained to "go" only on its T-stand or in its cage is a real advantage. The bird owner must, however, be more involved in the process than the dog owner. Most dogs will whine at the door or otherwise alert the owner that a discreet excursion is required. Parrots don't announce their needs quite so directly. So even with a toilet-trained parrot, we need to be alert for the signs.

It is important to know that the length of a parrot's digestive tract has a direct bearing on how often it will have to deposit its droppings. The time it takes for food just eaten to make its way in the form of digested waste to the vent is much shorter for small birds, like budgies and cockatiels, than for medium-sized and large parrots, such as African Greys, Amazons, macaws, and cockatoos. This is why it is easier to toilet train a large bird: They simply don't have to go as often, therefore not requiring the owner to be constantly jumping up and down to transport the bird to the designated toilet area.

Essentials of Toilet Training

To toilet train a parrot means to train it to eliminate in a specific place, rather than indiscriminately wherever it happens to be.

There are several things to consider in order to achieve the task:

- The area that will be used for the bird's toilet.

- The behavior that signals the parrot's need to defecate.

- Associating, in the parrot's mind, a selected word with the activity of elimination.

The owner should realize that in fact, it is we who become trained, rather than the parrot, although there are some birds that will eventually arrive at the point where they voluntarily go to the toileting area and may even verbalize their need.

You may elect to train your parrot to use a designated toileting area. It is also possible to teach a parrot to go on command. This is especially convenient when you have the bird a distance from the toileting area and can't get back quickly enough to avoid accidents. However, it may be confusing to the parrot to teach it both behaviors, because if it has learned to associate defecation with a particular area, eliminating on command wherever the owner takes it for this task may obliterate its desire to use the selected area.

It is probably wise to teach one or the other of the behaviors and stick with that method consistently.

The Toileting Area

This will be the place where it is acceptable for the parrot to deposit its droppings. You may decide the interior of the cage will be the spot, or it may be the parrot's play gym. Others may wish to use an easily cleaned surface such as a tiled floor. Alternately, you may hold the bird over the wastepaper can or the toilet.

Behavior Signaling the Need to Defecate

It is in this area that we become trained. In order to get the parrot to the right spot at the right time, we must learn to recognize when a dropping is on its way. Most birds will ruffle their feathers a bit. Squirming a little or a lot is also a tip-off. Some parrots will stop what they are doing and get a rather faraway look in the eye, very like human toddlers in the same situation. J.B., our Mealy Amazon, always grunts and shifts his left leg a little to the side. Other parrots will merely lift their tails slightly and nonchalantly let loose.

Observe your bird carefully to determine what combination of signals routinely precedes a dropping.

The Magic Word

Using the same word each time your parrot defecates eventually enables it to associate the word with the deed. This is particularly easy to do if you are hand-feeding a nestling. Babies usually defecate during or immediately after receiving a feeding. Every time this happens, remark in bright, enthusiastic tones, "A POO! (or whatever word you've chosen). What a lovely POO. Look, everyone, Polly just made a POO!" Praise the baby lavishly. (Yes, I know this sounds exactly like toilet training a human toddler, but what was it I said in an earlier chapter about parrots being very like young children?)

Doing the same thing with a newly weaned parrot or an adult is almost as easy. Every time the bird defecates in your presence, call its attention to the act with the chosen word and lavish praise.

Accidents

Inevitably there will be accidents. It is unreasonable to expect that a "toilet-trained" parrot will be as fastidious about its droppings as a cat or dog. For one thing, parrots defecate when they are frightened. It makes no difference where the bird happens to be at the time, or how reliable it usually is in its toilet habits. Fright defecation is a physiological response, and the parrot has little control over it.

Parrots also defecate when they alight after flying. Although your parrot's wing feathers have been trimmed—haven't they?—if you have been exercising your bird by having it flap its wings, it will surely defecate as soon as it is returned to perch, furniture, or elsewhere. This instinct, by the way, comes in very handy when training the bird to defecate on command.

Parrots fed an abundance of fresh vegetables and fruits must urinate more often than usual due to the high water content of their diet. This also causes an increase in the number and frequency of solid droppings. Warm weather will cause parrots to drink more often, with the same result. Illness may increase the frequency of droppings, as well.

It should go without saying that a parrot should *never* be punished for having toilet accidents. Doing so will not "teach the bird better." It will only create a frightened, aggressive animal that not only becomes impervious to your toilet training attempts, but to training of any kind.

Lavish great praise on your parrot when the deed is properly done. Ignore mistakes.

Defecation on Command or at the Toileting Area?

As mentioned previously, choose one method and then stick with it in order to avoid confusing your bird. I personally prefer to teach parrots defecation on command. It is more convenient for me periodically to encourage my birds to eliminate at a convenient place wherever we may be at the time. Running downstairs from the office to cage or perch is time-consuming and aggravating. This is a choice based on my lifestyle and responsibilities. Others may wish to choose the toilet area option. It is strictly the owner's choice. The parrot doesn't care one way or the other!

Whatever the choice, toilet training should be approached gently and with patience. It cannot be rushed, and miracles should not be expected overnight.

The object of toilet training is to reduce the number of droppings in unacceptable areas, thus eliminating extra cleanups and avoidable damage. Its purpose is not the creation of an anal-retentive parrot or a home totally free of droppings in the wrong places. Droppings *come with the territory*, as the saying goes. Alas for us parrot owners, droppings will always be with us, and damage containment is the true goal of toilet training our birds!

Defecation on Command

The first step in this method is associating, in the parrot's mind, the command word with the deed. When you feel your bird has grasped this concept, begin to watch it for the signs indicating a dropping is on its way in the immediate future. When you see them, take the parrot to a convenient spot (tile floor, waste can, T-stand, etc.). Hold the bird on your hand and give the word. (In our house, the word is "Poo.") Hold the bird in position until the dropping appears. If the parrot is reluctant to defecate, hold it on your hand and gently circle it through the air a few times to encourage wing flapping. When the flapping has stopped, give the command again. The parrot will inevitably defecate at this point, more or less because you have intervened. Praise the bird enthusiastically and return it to its previous location.

Repeat this process every time you are with the bird, being sure to watch carefully for the warning signals. In a shorter time than you might imagine, it will begin to defecate when you tell it to, where you want it to.

If a longer-than-usual period has elapsed without any indication the parrot needs to defecate, take it to a convenient area and give the command, using the wing flapping if necessary, to induce elimination. In this way, you are reinforcing the lesson at the same time you are preventing a potential "accident."

This method has worked so well for us that Mac, my Timneh Grey, reached the point where he absolutely never had his huge morning "poo" in his cage, but waited until he was uncovered and taken to the wastebasket. It saved a great deal of extra cage paper changing, and Mac always seemed rather proud of himself over his accomplishment.

J.B., our Mealy Amazon, never has an accident on my husband if Bill remembers to toilet him every forty-five minutes or so while he is holding him. J.B. is plunked down on the tile entryway and told to "poo." He casts adoring looks at my spouse, grunts, groans, shifts his leg, and obeys the command. Even if he only manages a little bit, he does it anyway. J.B. is a very good, very obliging parrot. Now—if we could only train him to mop up!

Our parrots are so conditioned to eliminate on command that if the other birds are within hearing range of one that has been told to "Poo," one of the others will often oblige. This can be a problem if parrot number two or three happens to be somewhere that droppings will not appreciated. However, one certainly has to applaud their desire to please.

Defecation at the Toileting Area

First, select the desired area. It should be a location that can be quickly reached when your bird indicates elimination is imminent, and it should lend itself to easy cleaning. You may need to establish a second toileting area, especially if you are frequently on another floor of the house and the parrot spends time there with you. This should not be a problem for the bird, as it can easily learn that when out of its cage, no matter where it is, there are specific areas in which to eliminate.

Second, learn what signals your parrot typically gives when it is about ready to deposit a dropping.

Third, if you have not already done so, observe your parrot as previously described and use the chosen potty word whenever it eliminates in your presence. When you feel the parrot recognizes the word and associates it with defecation, you are ready to proceed.

When your parrot indicates a dropping is on its way, pick up your parrot and place your hand over the tail base—thus preventing the necessary tail lifting that helps the bird accomplish the function. Then quickly carry it to the appointed toileting area. Place the parrot in the area and remove your hand from the tail. Give your chosen command word and let the parrot do the rest.

When your parrot does defecate, praise it lavishly and return with it to whatever you were both doing before bathroom duties called.

Repeat this program every time the bird is away from its cage and with you. Eventually, it will become conditioned to use only the toileting area. In time, many parrots will learn to tell their owners when they need to go by verbalizing the toilet command. This is a great help, but even if your parrot never does it, the fact that it is willing to use the appointed area a good portion of the time indicates that your training and patience have been amply rewarded.

What Has Been Learned in This Chapter?

- Parrots can be potty trained.

- It is somewhat easier to train a medium- or large-sized parrot than a small one, because small parrots need to defecate far more often.

- We ourselves must become trained if we are to toilet train our parrots successfully.

- There are two toilet training methods: elimination on command and elimination at a selected toileting area.

- We should choose which of the two methods to use and train only for the method of choice.

- We must familiarize ourselves with the signals that indicate the parrot needs to defecate.

- A "potty command" word or phrase must be chosen and used consistently.

- Toilet accidents will happen with the best-trained parrot; they should be ignored. Punishment of any kind should never be used when the parrot has an accident.

9

Speech Training

Where there is intelligence, there is knowledge.

—Greek proverb

Ever since parrots were first kept as companions, people have wondered if their birds could actually understand spoken language. Certainly, parrots do mimic. They like the sound of their own voices and will repeat favorite words and phrases simply for this reason.

However, many individual parrots *do* understand what they are saying and use their human speech vocabularies appropriately. This is supported by a large body of anecdotal material. In addition, the work of Dr. Irene M. Pepperberg of the University of Arizona gives every indication that parrots are capable of learning to use speech intelligently. Her work with Alex, an African Grey parrot, as well as two younger Greys she has recently included in her research, place this question—at least in the case of some individual parrots—far beyond speculation. Dr. Pepperberg's work has been published in many distinguished scientific journals and has credibility in the august halls of scientific inquiry.

We who have spent years with parrots are not surprised at this. We are indeed grateful that Dr. Pepperberg's research has supported what many of us have known all along. It is rather humbling to think that our parrots can, at least sometimes,

Acquisition of speech may add to the luster of your parrot.

truly communicate with us in what for them is a foreign language—not only a foreign language, but one that crosses species barriers!

We cannot communicate in "parrotese." Nor can we fly. In fact, we humans are largely incapable of entering into the realm of animal thinking and being, except in a purely deductive and imaginative way. But these highly intelligent creatures we call parrots, beings we often think of as belonging to an order several magnitudes below human evolutionary status, have done what we cannot.

Not long ago, Gunny, my Blue and Gold Macaw, was perched on my arm while I was getting a glass of water. Gunny is a mellow fellow, but human speech is not his strong point. He has a few English words, which he uses appropriately from time to time. His Spanish vocabulary is larger, because before he came to me following the death of our son, he had spent time with a local Hispanic family. As I turned on the tap, he suddenly said, "What's that?" I replied that "it" was water. He then looked at me (rather earnestly, I thought, but that could just have been a fanciful interpretation) and said, "Want some." I looked at him with a great deal of surprise, because in the seven years he has been with us, he had never given rein to such a "purposeful" verbal exchange. Gunny continued to look at me and then the running water. I filled a small paper cup and offered it to him. He took several large swigs, then wiped his beak on my arm, apparently satisfied that I had gotten the point. (It would have been hard not to!)

Another example of intelligent, appropriate speech comes to mind. Chico is an African Grey parrot with a gift for cognitive speech. She belongs to Gayle Soucek and her husband, Peter Rimsa. For whatever reason, Chico calls Pete "Joe." No matter how many times Gayle and Pete have tried to get the parrot to call Pete by his proper name, she persists in using her own name for him. One evening, Gayle and Pete were deep in earnest, serious conversation. Chico wanted Pete's undivided attention and began to call, at first softly and then more loudly, "Joe! Joe!" This went on for several minutes, until Pete, exasperated with Chico's persistent demands, said crossly, "Chico, hush up and leave me alone. I'm busy!" Chico looked at him and "almost rolled her eyes," according to Gayle. Then she turned her back on Pete and muttered in annoyed tones, "*Crabby* Joe!"

Hannah is a White-capped *Pionus* with whom I am privileged to live. She was presented to me by a dear friend, who is also a breeder, as a companion for a Ring-necked parakeet who will never be able to have a mate of his species, owing to his extremely timid nature and the extreme aggressiveness of Ring-necked hens. Hannah is a little princess with a rather elevated opinion of herself. She is also a gifted talker, picking up words and phrases with ease. She had been with us about eighteen months, when one day I was in the aviary cleaning and feeding. I heard her say something that sounded like "Good morning, Aunt Bonnie." Hannah had been saying "Good morning, punkin" for months. I say this to my birds every morning when I enter the aviary, but I had never heard her say "Aunt Bonnie." Obviously, I don't call myself Aunt Bonnie. When I do refer to myself around the birds, I always call myself "Mom." Nor does my husband call me Aunt Bonnie. (If he did, I think I'd be seriously disturbed!) In short, Hannah had never heard me called that, ever under any circumstance. Well, I was startled, but thought at the time the little parrot might have been mumbling something else and I had misheard her. However, the next few days proved me wrong, when I strolled into the aviary and she looked me in the eye and caroled, "Good morning, Aunt Bonnie! How are you, sweetheart?"

My husband didn't believe me, but a few days later when he heard it with his own ears, he was forced to admit that our little Hannah had pulled a verbal rabbit out of the hat. Finally, consumed with curiosity, I asked Pam Willis, Hannah's breeder, if Hannah had ever heard her refer to me as Aunt Bonnie. Pam thought a while, then replied that she might have said that once or twice shortly before she brought Hannah to me. She had said words to the effect that pretty soon Hannah would be going to live with Aunt Bonnie—but only once or twice. And yet eighteen months later, after having heard my husband call me Bonnie, Hannah put it all together, deciding I must be *the* Aunt Bonnie she'd been told about!

Then there is Singletary, Eli's mate. It has been a long time now since Singletary called Eli by anything other than his given name. When she is sitting eggs and becomes alarmed for any reason, she hollers "Eli!" in a way that puts her big, ferocious, devoted mate into an immediate flurry of aggressive protectiveness. It is no wonder that parrots sometimes present behavioral challenges; that they are often cleverly manipulative; that they sometimes defy our ability to understand and relate to them constructively; that in many cases, it is difficult if not impossible to deny their understanding of human language. Their ancient, often unknowable, mystique is a large part of their appeal for us.

Can all parrots learn to speak with understanding and intent? Probably not. Can some parrots learn this skill? Undoubtedly. Can *your* parrot learn this kind of speech? That depends on a combination of the individual bird's traits and its owner's. Many separate factors must exist for this to happen.

Can your parrot learn to mimic human speech? Almost certainly, if you will make the commitment to training. Some parrots will learn only a few words; others will be able to develop astounding vocabularies. Some will have beautifully clear speech, while some will mumble so badly that only their owners will be able to understand them.

Is it necessary that your parrot talk? Not really. This acquired skill, while adding to the shine of your bird's personality and presence, will not alter its personality. It is "frosting on the cake," so to speak, because the true shimmer and glow of having a parrot is the relationship between bird and human. There have been many beloved pet parrots that never uttered a word. There have also been talented talkers who disdained even a minimal relationship with their humans, for whatever reason. Of course, there have been parrots without number who were not only dear pets, but entertained, amused, touched, and dazzled their proud humans with feats of verbal magic.

Which Parrots Are Most Likely to Talk?

Although most parrot species have the potential to learn at least one or two words, some have made it to the "Parrot Language Hall of Fame." The African Grey is the species most widely known and admired for its ability to talk and imitate a human voice—so closely that its voice cannot be distinguished from that of the person being mimicked.

African Greys often do not begin talking until close to their first birthdays or slightly after. They seem to spend the time up to this point listening and babbling, practicing various speech sounds. Once they do begin, it may seem as if a floodgate has opened, though the more usual pattern is a steady, sure acquisition of words and phrases over time. Owners of African Greys should be aware that because these parrots are high-strung, it is extremely unusual for them to talk in front of strangers. So regardless of how talented a talker your Grey becomes, be prepared for a total mute when you attempt to show off its vocal skills for guests.

After the African Grey (as a talker par excellence) come the Amazons. There are many species of Amazon parrots, but the ones most likely to become talented talkers are of the *ochrocephala* group. This group includes Yellow-naped, Yellow-fronted, and Double Yellow-headed Amazons. Although not an *ochrocephala* species, the Blue-headed Amazon is also a talented talker. Amazons are outgoing, gregarious birds, and the presence of strangers usually will not inhibit their speech.

Budgerigars, affectionately known as "budgies" and often, though wrongly, called parakeets, are excellent talkers. Although their voices are tiny, making one wish they could be hooked up to amplifiers in some way, they can amass an astounding vocabulary. I am reminded of a budgie owned by the daughter of a former neighbor. This good lady, cultured and etiquette-bound, was horrified one day to hear the little parrot address a guest she was entertaining to tea in clarion tones, "You stink!" Elizabeth's daughter had been teaching her budgie to speak American slang, much to her mother's distress.

Macaws can be very good talkers. Those domestically bred seem to be more proficient than their earlier, wild counterparts. Their diction, however, is apt to be a little less clear than that of some species.

Cockatoos can be good talkers, but their very poor diction often makes them difficult to understand. Of course, there are exceptions to this. Among the cockatoos, the little Bare-eyed Cockatoo is an excellent talker, with clear pronunciation and the ability to learn many words and phrases.

Cockatiels often learn to speak well. They are also talented whistlers, and many are able to learn to whistle tunes with ease. As with the budgie, their speaking voices are small. Their whistling can be quite loud and shrill, however.

Although this handful of species has gained a well-deserved reputation for learning to talk well, there are differences in ability among individuals. Even if your parrot does not belong to this illustrious group with a high potential for speech, do not be discouraged from trying to teach your bird to talk. Remember, most parrots have the ability to pick up a few words, provided the owner is willing to work with them on a daily, consistent basis. Even if your parrot never ascends to the heights of an avian William Jennings Bryan or a Sir Laurence Olivier, speech training is an excellent way to further the human/parrot bond. Those few words learned will mean more to you (and possibly your parrot) than another parrot's ability to recite the Gettysburg Address, because you worked at reaching its accomplishment together!

Some parrots just never do learn to talk. Our Miss Molly, though a dear little soul, has never spoken a word, but we love her anyway. Actually, considering the fact that she is something of an airhead, perhaps it's just as well that she confines her verbalization to her particular cockatoo dialect. On the other hand, Miss Molly can understand and follow fairly long, complex verbal instructions, so her lack of human speech does not reflect any lack of intelligence, or an inability to understand human speech. Maybe Molly isn't such an airhead after all.

How Do Parrots Learn to Speak?

Basically, parrots learn to speak much as human infants do. The learning process involves listening, practicing, and repetition. This is especially true for the parrot that mimics. The process of repetition also has its place if you are working to teach your parrot cognitive (understood and appropriately used) speech.

The progress to spoken language is orderly and predictable. In the first stage, the parrot merely listens and absorbs. You can watch your parrot doing this. When you or other family members speak, the parrot will often fix its attention unwaveringly on the speaker for a time. It may cock its head or give other indications of its interest. Adults as well as weanlings and nestlings do this. Words and sentences spoken with special vigor will nearly always get their undivided attention. (This is why so many birds pick up profanities easily. When you live with a parrot with good talking potential, you must watch your language, just as with a young child. A parrot with an "X-rated" vocabulary eventually becomes tiresome and may turn into a real liability, none of which is actually its fault, but the fault of careless owners.)

Second comes the process of experimenting with sounds. You will usually hear your bird mumbling and babbling to itself as it tries various combinations of vowels and consonants. This is precisely what human toddlers do when they are learning to speak.

The third and last stage in language acquisition is the actual verbalization of recognizable words, clearly enunciated. At this stage, the parrot may or may not associate the word with an object or action, depending on its individual talent and mental powers. Actually, toddlers at this stage may not always connect what they are saying with whatever it is the word symbolizes. There is a technique that you may use to help this process with your parrot. Parents use it all the time with their little ones, without realizing what they are doing because it is so natural.

This technique is called *referential mapping*, a two-dollar word for a million-dollar aid to developing intelligent speech. It works like this: Say, for example, Polly seems to be trying to say "Apple," something she's heard you say time and again as you offer her a piece of this fruit. The word is a little garbled, but you're pretty sure this is what's going on. Your response would then be, as you offer the apple, "Apple. This is apple, Polly. Apple is good. Apple." Do this often enough, and Polly will begin to use the word specifically to identify an apple, or even to request one. The same thing happens when a parent sees his toddler pointing to the cookie jar and saying something that at least starts with a hard "C" sound. "Do you want a cookie, Timmy? Does Timmy want a cookie?" If Dad follows through with a cookie, then Timmy pretty quickly learns that saying this word will produce a lovely treat of the cookie variety every time he says the word out.

Because the basis of speaking any language rests on the opportunity to hear it spoken first, we emphasize again the importance of enriching your parrot's environment, especially regarding language. As your bird hears you and other family members speak, and watches and listens to television or radio talk shows with you, its mind will be storing the sounds and cadences of human speech. When you read aloud to it, the same thing happens. When you speak not *to* it, but *with* it, as you would with a young child, this process happens. Talking with your parrot—sharing your day, your problems, your goals and hopes—will not only foster bonding, but includes the parrot in your life in a way that may foster its desire to communicate with you. We cannot support this supposition with data, but experience seems to bear it out. It may have something to do with the fact that parrots are social flock animals, and it is natural for them to want to communicate with other flock members, even if they are human rather than avian.

There are various kinds of speech training you may pursue with your parrot, but essential to all is allowing your bird to hear human speech on a regular, consistent, fairly intense basis. It also helps to have, or be in the process of fostering, a close bond with your bird.

Use of Prerecorded Training Devices

Audiotapes, compact disc recordings, and phonograph records, all offering a quick, easy way to teach your parrot to talk, are widely available today. These, however, have one common drawback limiting their effectiveness: The parrot/owner relationship, with all that means in terms of successfully teaching your bird to talk, is missing. Because of this, these devices are not recommended if you are serious about teaching Polly to speak the human language.

One electronic technique, the endless loop audiocassette, may be helpful as a supportive aid. These cassettes are available for use in some kinds of telephone answering machines. The thirty-second tape is most useful by allowing the owner to record, in his or her own voice, the word or phrase currently being taught. You have only to say whatever it is four or five times, in a clear, distinct voice. When placed in a tape player, the tape cycles repeatedly, for as long as you wish it to play. If you use an appliance timer in conjunction with the tape player, especially one that is programmed to allow multiple on/off settings, you can play the recording you have made two or three times a day for fifteen to thirty minutes. This may prove helpful to reinforce one-on-one sessions with your parrot, especially if you are out during the day. Be careful not to play the tape so often for so long that it becomes meaningless background noise, with the result that the parrot tunes it out.

In any case, use of an endless loop cassette recording should never take the place of personal speech training sessions with your bird.

The Training Area

Speech training should take place twice a day for ten or fifteen minutes. Setting a timer will ensure that you are not skimping on the time spent. This is easy to do, because it can get mighty boring sitting in one place for a length of time, repeating the same word or phrase over and over.

Before starting your training sessions, select an area in your home that will be quiet and free of distractions. A bedroom is ideal for this. Children yelling and playing, dogs barking, or televisions, stereos, and radios blaring all make it impossible to hold your parrot's attention. Using a bathroom, even a second or third one, is not recommended, because almost inevitably as soon as you and your bird are comfortably settled and absorbed in the lesson, someone in the family will have the need to use it.

There are some myths about teaching a parrot to talk. One is that the cage should be covered with the parrot in it during the lesson; another is that the bird should be placed in a dark closet. Both of these originate with the notion that the parrot should be free of distractions. This is true, but it is not necessary or advisable to cover the cage or place the bird in the dark. It will learn far better perched on your arm or hand in a quiet area, enjoying your company, your undivided attention, and its lesson.

There are some times of the day when the parrot will be in a more vocal mood, and thus naturally inclined to attend and eventually try to imitate what you are attempting to teach it. These times are in the early morning and in the evening, just around dusk. If at all possible, try to schedule speech lessons during these periods.

Patience and General Guidelines

Teaching your parrot to say its first two or three words is a long, potentially frustrating experience. The bird will be absorbing and trying to learn totally new ways of vocalizing, using syllables, vowels, and consonants completely foreign to its usual mode of communication. Without patience and faith that you and the parrot can accomplish the desired goal, nothing will happen.

Several weeks, or even months, may elapse before the thrilling moment when you hear your bird trying to say the magic word. When the time comes, you probably will hear Polly mumbling something that sounds suspiciously like what you've been trying to teach her. At first, you may decide that after all this time, your imagination is playing tricks on you. As Polly's diction becomes more and more clear, you will no longer be able to deny that the momentous time has arrived: Polly is honest-to-goodness talking! It's a great day.

Some parrots will learn faster than others, and some seem to take forever. Some birds will already have a word or two prior to formal speech lessons. This is particularly true of certain hand-reared species.

Regardless of the parrot's potential ability, start lessons with a simple word such as "Hello" or "Hi." Save long phrases or difficult words for when Polly is already talking well. Parrots generally learn to repeat sounds they like. If you've drilled for weeks and no results are forthcoming, try a new word. As odd as it seems, I was never able to teach Mac, my Timneh Grey, to say anything derogatory about himself. I tried for months to teach him to say, "I'm a little devil." It was simply no use. Mac had far too good an opinion of himself to cast aspersions on his own character!

Since parrots learn words and phrases that appeal to them more easily than those that don't, make your rendition of the word as dramatic as possible (without frightening the parrot, of course). Avoid monotones and lackluster delivery, sometimes difficult to do when you've repeated a word a hundred times in a single session. If you watch your parrot carefully during training sessions, you will be able to gauge its degree of interest in the word and your manner of saying it by the way its pupils contract and dilate. This indicates interest and excitement and is a very good sign. If, on the other hand, Polly stares off into space with all the interest of a high school sophomore at a calculus lecture, either change your delivery or the word or phrase.

Never try to teach two or more different, unrelated words or phrases during the same time period. Choose one word and stick with it until your parrot is able to repeat it successfully, or until you've decided that this particular word is never going to be a part of Polly's lexicon.

Generally speaking, once a parrot has mastered two or three words, it will take less time to teach subsequent words and phrases. Many parrots will begin to pick up words on their own, as well.

Three Methods of Speech Training

The following are the most commonly used methods of training a parrot to speak. Before proceeding further, however, let's address the old wives' tale about how splitting a parrot's tongue makes it a better talker. This is absolutely untrue. It is cruel; it does not work; and no veterinarian worth his or her diploma would even consider it.

The first method is training the parrot to mimic. The second is teaching responsive speech, in which the owner poses a question and the bird responds with the correct answer. This method, too, is basically teaching the parrot to mimic and respond on cue. It works best if the parrot already has some mimicked speech. The third method is to teach the parrot cognitive speech. This method involves the use of the Model/Rival technique, perfected by the distinguished Dr. Irene M. Pepperberg in her work with Alex.

All three methods require time and patience, but cognitive training is perhaps the most demanding. It also requires the participation of two people, although it is not necessary that they be the same people every time. It is only necessary that the human participants be familiar with the principles involved and not deviate from them.

Teaching a Parrot to Mimic Speech

This is the basic technique most commonly used to train parrots to talk. It can also serve as a beginning tool for those who wish to progress to responsive and cognitive speech training. This method teaches the parrot to develop its attention span. It provides a way to further the human/parrot bond (as indeed all types of training do), and it usually results in the parrot's acquisition of human words and phrases.

Before starting any speech training session, put away cares and worries and try to be as relaxed as possible—just as you would for any training session. Remember that both you and the parrot should be having fun doing this. True, it can become boring if you allow it; but if you find boredom creeping in, keep in mind the goal and the pleasure success will bring you both.

It is certainly permissible to stop the session briefly to get up and stroll around the room with your bird, talking to it in conversational tones, perhaps looking out a window or playing together briefly. This sort of thing refreshes the mind of human and parrot alike. Mac used to love it when I put him down on the bed and played a modified sort of tag with him. Whatever brings a short period of respite that allows you both to return to the task at hand refreshed will make the lessons more effective in the long run. Just don't spend most of your time playing, because you will defeat the purpose of the training sessions.

When the time has come for a training session, proceed in this fashion:

- Set a timer for ten or fifteen minutes, whichever time period better suits you and your parrot's attention span.

- Take the parrot on your hand or arm to the training area.

- When you arrive at the training area, seat yourself comfortably on a bed or chair.

- Keep the parrot on your hand or arm. Do not allow it to climb to your shoulder or hop off and wander.

- With the bird positioned so you can make eye contact with it and it can see your lips, slowly and clearly pronounce the word you wish to teach the parrot.

- Continue repeating the word over and over, watching carefully for the parrot's reaction and signs that its attention is wandering.

- Take a brief break if circumstances indicate you should.

- At the end of the training session, praise and pet the parrot and return it to its cage. A small treat at this time is perfectly appropriate.

- Have fun!

When your parrot has successfully mastered the word or phrase being taught, stop the speech training for a few days, while at the same time taking every opportunity to reinforce its newly acquired skill. Praise your parrot whenever you hear it repeat what you have taught it.

After a few days or a week, you may start again with a new word. Begin each training session repeating the previously learned word a time or two, then go on to bigger and better things!

Teaching Responsive Speech

This is a variation of speech mimicry. It should not be attempted before the parrot has learned a few words through the speech mimicry method previously discussed.

The object is to teach the parrot to respond with a desired word or phrase in response to a statement or question made to it. For example, you may wish to teach the parrot to say its name when you ask "What's your name?" Or you may want the bird to say "Hangin' out," when you ask, "Whatcha doin'?" The choice is as wide as your imagination and the parrot's ability to learn the desired response. It helps to keep the response as short and simple as possible. As with teaching ordinary speech mimicry, expect to invest considerable time in order to achieve desired results.

When teaching responsive speech, it is helpful to use a small, nutritious food treat as a reward. Because of this, teaching this particular skill may go more quickly if Polly has not eaten for a while. This method of speech training has a good deal in common with trick training, in that you will be teaching a conditioned response. When teaching conditioned responses, food is the reward of choice.

If you are feeding twice a day, morning and evening, you may want to work with this method just before breakfast or dinner is served. The evening, an hour or two after the parrot has eaten, may also work well for you. Under no circumstance should the parrot be deprived of food for the purpose of teaching responsive speech. Rather, choose your training time as it relates to the parrot's daily routine. This training time should be the same time every day.

Although you may wish to begin the training in the usual area, eventually you will be working with the bird in the area where it generally spends time, as it will be learning to make the appropriate response wherever it is, whenever the question is asked.

In this method, the response is taught first. Taking one of the previous examples, Polly will be learning to say "Hangin' out":

- When you are settled with the parrot in the training area, show the treat, then slowly and clearly say, "Hangin' out."

- As soon as Polly begins to attempt saying the phrase, praise and reward her with the treat. As her pronunciation becomes clearer, praise and reward. Do not reward for garbled or unclear speech after you are sure she can do better.

When Polly has mastered the response, move into the cage area (if you were not already there) and begin working with her there, following the above instructions. There may be a bit of backsliding because of ordinary household activities and being in or near her cage. When she once again is making the appropriate response on cue (being shown the treat), you are ready to begin the second phase of training:

- Begin training at the usual time.

- When you approach Polly, show her the treat and ask her, "Whatcha doin'?" Because she has been conditioned to give the response when shown the reward, and because you have consistently worked with her on this skill at the same time every day, she may very well respond the first time with "Hangin' out." If this happens, praise and reward her.

- If Polly does not "get it," continue asking your question. Be prepared for a long wait. These things take time. Reward only for the desired word or phrase. Do not reward if Polly volunteers the response before the question has been asked.

- When Polly at last makes the appropriate response at the appropriate time, praise and reward.

- Continue drilling until the response to your question becomes reflexive and automatic.

At this point, you are ready to begin the third phase of responsive speech training. You will do this by moving farther and farther away from your parrot when you ask the question. When you both have arrived at the point where no matter where you and Polly are, she responds correctly to your question, your task has been accomplished. Continue to praise her lavishly for performing correctly.

At some point, you can eliminate the treat if you wish, using praise as the sole reward. This is largely a decision based on your parrot's personality. Some birds are more than willing to continue performing correctly with verbal praise and affection as their sole reward; others would rather "work for their tummies." Determine what works better for your parrot. If there is some reluctance to perform correctly when food rewards are withdrawn, there is no harm in reinstituting them as a motivator.

Teaching Cognitive Speech

This is the *sine qua non* of speech training for the apt parrot. Regrettably, not many people use this method with their birds, though it is not particularly difficult to use. As with any other training method, it requires commitment from the owner, as well as an understanding of the methods and underlying principles. It also requires a great deal of time.

Although I will go into detail here on the requirements and methods for using this technique successfully, the reader can also acquire Dr. Pepperberg's videotape on the method. This tape can be ordered from Avian Publications (6381 Monroe Street Northeast, Minneapolis, MN 55432; 1-800-577-BIRD). As well as providing a feel for this method that will greatly enhance your chances of success with your feathered bundle of brilliance, part of the cost of the video goes to the Alex Fund, which supports Dr. Pepperberg's excellent work. For those of you who are not yet familiar with Dr. Pepperberg's research and teaching methods, you have a very special treat in store. And you will be amazed at what can be accomplished by a committed teacher and a willing pupil!

You will note that I have used the word "teach" rather than "train" with respect to this technique, which is called the Model/Rival technique. That is because you will indeed be teaching—teaching your parrot to use its considerable intelligence to learn to use human language with accuracy and intent. If running the equivalent of an avian kindergarten for your parrot, with all of its joys, frustrations, and incomparable rewards, is your heart's desire, this is the method for you!

When using this method, it is not necessary to have used mimicry or responsive speech training first nor are food treats used as rewards, except in very special circumstances, which will be discussed later.

Using this method involves three participants. One person is the teacher. The second person is the pupil—that's right, the pupil! The third individual is the parrot, whose role is that of an observer at some times and a participant at others. The two people do not have to be the same two all of the time, but it probably helps to have at least one of the individuals present for most of the sessions.

It is also important to note that the role of teacher and pupil are switched around on a regular basis, even within the same training session. This teaches the parrot that questions, correct responses, and interactions are not dependent on only one person or one circumstance, but can change frequently without the teaching content being altered. It comes to realize that "what is, is," regardless of circumstances. For example, corn is corn, whether Mom asks the question and Dad answers, or Dad asks the question and Junior answers. Basically, the parrot learns that words are symbols of objects or actions in the real world and can be used to communicate meaningfully in any situation. If that boggles your mind, you're in good company. Dr. Pepperberg's research is impeccable, and her results are beyond doubt. Her method works, and there is no reason why it can't work for others, as long as there is understanding of the method and consistency on the part of the human participants.

The training area and equipment are simple but, as with the previous two methods, should provide a distraction-free environment and comfort for humans as well as parrot. Two chairs are needed, as well as a comfortable perch for the parrot. A T-stand is highly recommended. The chairs should be positioned facing each other—one for the teacher, the other for the pupil. The T-stand should be placed so the parrot can see, and be close to, teacher and pupil.

Props will consist of whatever is being taught. If, for example, you are going to teach Polly to say "carrot" and associate the word with that worthy vegetable, then small pieces of carrot *must* be on hand. This is one of the two major components of the Model/Rival teaching method. The parrot receives as its reward the object it learns to say. In this way, it is able to associate in its mind the word symbol for an actual object, color, texture, and so forth. Food is never the reward unless you are teaching the parrot the name of a particular food.

The second of the two major components of the Model/Rival technique is that it is an interactive situation in real context. The parrot sees the interaction between the "pupil" receiving the "teacher's" attention and will want to compete and participate.

A further word about props is necessary. If you are going to teach colors, use several objects of the color being taught. In this way, the parrot will learn to recognize "blue" (or any other color) as a color no matter what object it adorns.

Using the Model/Rival technique, you can teach Polly to recognize shapes— "What shape, Polly?"—as you present a triangle, square, or circle. Dr. Pepperberg has taught Alex to identify shape by the number of corners present: a triangle, for example, has three corners. You can teach names of food and other objects— "What object, Polly?"—as you show her a grape, a key, or a walnut. That which can be taught using this technique is limited only by your imagination, ingenuity, time commitment, and patience.

Let's look at a sample teaching session. You (Beth, for the sake of the example) and your husband (George) are seated in chairs facing each other. Polly is on her T-stand, positioned in such a way that she can easily see you both, as well as the object or concept being taught. The area is quiet and free of distractions. You have decided to teach Polly to say "grape" and to use the word properly and in context. This may take several days or even a few weeks; progress will not happen overnight. As you continue working with this technique and Polly's vocabulary and appropriate use of what she has learned expand, progress will likely be a little faster.

> **Beth, showing the grape to George:** "This object GRAPE, George. Grape." Places grape in her mouth. "GRAPE is good!" Holds up another grape. "GRAPE."

> George looks with interest at the grape.

> **Beth continues to hold the grape for George's inspection:** "What object, George?"

> **George:** Mumbles something unintelligible.

> **Beth:** "GRAA . . . PE. GRAA . . . PE.

> **George:** "Gruhhh. Gruhhh."

> **Beth:** "That's right, George! GRAA . . . PE. GRAPE." Hands the grape to George, who eats it.

> **Beth:** "GRAPE is good! Do you want another GRAPE?"

> **George:** "Gruh."

> **Beth:** "More clearly, George. You can say it more clearly. GRAA . . . PE."

> **George:** "Gray."

> **Beth:** "That's right, George, GRAPE." Hands George the grape, and he eats it with enthusiasm.

At this point, Beth and George switch roles and go through the whole exercise again. After this has been done, either person may take on the role of teacher and this time, Polly will be the pupil and the second person will be the observer. The teacher will (1) explain what the object is; (2) demonstrate how it is used (it is eaten); (3) comment on the object ("good"); (4) reward Polly with the object when Polly attempts to say the word; and (5) as the parrot progresses, reward her with the object only when pronunciation is acceptably clear.

The above example is necessarily condensed for reasons of space. In real time, it may be several days before Polly attempts to say the word representing the object, and her diction may be garbled. If Polly says another word she has learned, in the hope that this will bring her the reward of a succulent grape, the teacher will correct her: "No, Polly. Not carrot. Object is GRAPE. GRAPE."

Switching teacher/pupil/observer roles, along with saying the word symbol in a meaningful way ("GRAPE is good. Yum!"), helps the parrot learn that the word is indeed a symbol and can be used to ask for or identify the object or action desired. This is the basis for teaching it to use speech appropriately and intelligently.

When teaching shapes, the teacher should show the object and explain "three-corner," "two-corner" (a small dowel can be used for this one), and so forth. Properties like dullness or shininess, softness or hardness, should be similarly demonstrated. When teaching the parrot to ask for an object, the teacher should ask, "George, WANT X, Y, Z?" George's correct response will, at least at first, be "Grape." When Polly becomes the pupil, the same question and response will be used. Eventually, Polly will begin to associate the word "want" with whatever object is desired at the time and begin making her wishes known on the subject!

This is obviously a time-consuming teaching technique. However, for those who choose to use it, the likely eventual rewards will be greater than those attained by use of the other speech techniques presented. It is a purely personal choice on the owner's part as to which technique to use. None is "right" or "wrong." The main thing is to enjoy the process of training or teaching your parrot to use human language. Some owners will not wish to teach their parrots to speak at all. Parrots of those species with good potential for talking will probably pick up a few words even if they are never formally taught anything. In the last analysis, whether the parrot talks is not the truest measure of its value as a companion.

What Has Been Learned in This Chapter?

- Most parrots have the potential to acquire at least a few words.

- Some parrots are capable of learning to use speech appropriately and intelligently.

- Parrots do not need to learn how to talk to be good companions.

- Parrots of some species have greater potential for learning to talk than do others; but even within these groups, ability will vary, depending upon the individual parrot.

- Parrots acquire words in much the same way that human youngsters do.

- Working one-on-one with your parrot to teach it to talk is more effective than using tapes, CDs, or records.

- Great patience, consistency, and a suitable training area are required if one is to be successful in teaching a parrot to talk.

- The three basic techniques for teaching a parrot to talk are mimicry training, responsive speech training, and the Model/Rival technique perfected by Dr. Irene M. Pepperberg of the University of Arizona.

10

Trick Training

The devil finds work for idle beaks.

—Ancient parrot owner's proverb

Why teach your parrot tricks? Many pet owners avoid doing so because they feel that somehow, trick training a parrot detracts from the bird's natural dignity and nobility as a creature of nature. Certainly, trick training is not essential for a well-behaved parrot.

However, there are at least two good reasons to teach your parrot tricks. First, many owners and birds enjoy working together at this particular endeavor; it enhances the human/parrot bond. The second reason—and more important from the standpoint of this book—is that some parrots are extraordinarily active and intelligent. Parrots of this type tend to be manipulative and can be somewhat aggressive. They also have the potential to suffer great boredom, as they have few outlets for their restlessness and their active, boisterous, personalities.

Trick training for such parrots serves to channel mental and physical energy and to alleviate boredom. It provides mental stimulation and goal-oriented tasks that earn the parrot the attention and praise of its humans. Active birds thrive on this attention. If you have such a parrot, in addition to training the Three Basic Obedience Skills and/or working on various behavior problems mentioned in chapter 6, trick training may be a valuable tool to produce a delightfully well-behaved, happy, and accomplished bird. Trick training—as with any formal daily training program carried out consistently, following set guidelines, with specific goals in mind—enhances the human/parrot bond.

171

When training your parrot to perform a trick, use a carefully designed program with the same steps at every session. Conduct at least one daily training session, two being better. The sessions should not exceed the parrot's attention span. For some birds, this may be as short as ten minutes; others may work happily for up to a half hour. It is best to start with a ten- or fifteen-minute session, increasing its length if your parrot indicates a longer session will be tolerated and productive. Take care not to exceed the parrot's attention span and interest. It is most important to end the session on a high note, with the parrot still interested and willing to go on. This ensures that the bird continues to look forward to trick training time eagerly, rather than with dread or boredom.

Operant Conditioning

Teaching tricks uses a technique called operant conditioning. Simply, this means that an animal is taught to perform an action for a reward. The animal's learned behavior is called the conditioned response.

To produce a conditioned response, the animal must learn to associate the desired response with a reward of some kind. For example, if you are teaching your parrot to shake "hands," every time the bird makes a move in the right direction, such as lifting a foot when it hears the command "Shake," it should be given a small tidbit. Soon the parrot will begin to associate the food reward with the command and give the desired response.

All trainers use what is called a secondary reward, or "bridge," to signal that the action has been performed correctly and a food reward is forthcoming. Sometimes this secondary bridge may be a small metal "clicker." More frequently, it will be praise: "Good!" or "Okay!" or some other short, enthusiastic word or phrase. Because it is easy and natural to want to tell your parrot when it has done well, giving verbal praise is probably better than using a clicker.

Food Rewards

Although the use of food as a reward is discouraged when teaching the Three Basic Obedience Skills, it becomes necessary when trick training. Although many parrot trick behaviors are spin-offs of natural behavior (waving its wings on command, for example), they are still unnatural in that they would not be a part of the bird's normal behavior. It therefore becomes necessary that the parrot see some benefit to itself for cooperating in the training process.

The food reward should be a favorite of the parrot. Good items are hulled sunflower seeds and small pieces of "neat" fruit like apples or halved grapes. Small pieces of walnut will also work well. Mac adored wheat wafers and these, broken into very small pieces, worked well in his training. Small bits of cheese are also a good choice. Pre-packaged, coarsely shredded cheese is convenient and keeps well.

The operative word here is "small." The parrot should not be so gorged on treats that it shuns its regular diet. Small bits also whet its appetite for more, thus helping motivate it to work properly and attentively.

Training will also be facilitated if your parrot is slightly hungry. However, the bird should *never* be starved as a motivation to work for food. This is cruel and unnecessary, and it can lead to health problems. However, if Polly is feeling a bit "peckish," she will be a bit more willing to work at her trick for the food reward. Of course, some parrots are bottomless pits and will work just as well on a full tummy as on one that is somewhat empty. Know your bird's habits and preferences, and let them guide your decision.

Cues

The cue is the command given to the parrot: "Shake," "Dance," "Ring on the spindle," etc. It is important to use the same cue or command each time. Avoid saying, for example, "Shake hands, Polly" at one time, and the next time merely saying "Shake." Using different commands for the same trick will only cause confusion and slow progress. The cue should always be short and pointed. Long phrases are lost on parrots and again, progress will be slow or won't happen at all.

The Training Area

This area will be a little different from that used for training obedience skills. However, it should still be a relatively quiet, distraction-free area.

For some tricks, like waving, shaking hands, dancing, or nodding, the T-stand will be fine. For tricks that involve props, such as assembling puzzle pieces, placing coins in a bank, or rolling over, a table or the floor must be used. A table large enough to hold necessary props and allow the parrot to be comfortable and secure, is recommended because unlike the floor, the table allows the owner to control the parrot's movements. If the parrot is on the floor, boredom or curiosity may motivate it to scamper off with the owner in hot pursuit. Although amusing and fun for Polly, no learning can take place and the owner is apt to wind up frustrated and discouraged.

Equipment and Props

These consist of the items needed to teach the parrot the trick. If you are going to teach your parrot to put puzzle pieces in place correctly, have the puzzle on the training table and ready to go before bringing the bird to the table. Putting coins in the bank requires a piggy bank with a large slot and large coins, such as quarters, or poker chips. You must be sure to have enough coins for the entire session. And be sure the piggy bank has an opening so you can retrieve the loot after the training session; otherwise this particular trick could be mighty costly!

Some props, such as puzzles, must be modified to fit the parrot's needs. Puzzles should be made of wood or pressed board. The pieces should be large, simple, and colorful. Children's stores, especially those specializing in early childhood learning toys, are good places to find Polly's kind of puzzle. Large cup hooks should be screwed into each puzzle piece so the parrot can grasp the piece with ease. Most parrots will use their beaks for this task, but some, especially cockatoos, may use their feet.

If you are going to teach Polly to haul up a bucket for the treat at the bottom, the bucket should be small and light. The rope to which it is attached should be sturdy and easily grasped. For this purpose, old-fashioned cotton clothesline is best. If you can't locate cotton clothesline, multiple-twist nylon line of half-inch thickness works well. Avoid plastic clothesline. The diameter is too small, and its slick surface makes it difficult for parrots to grasp efficiently.

When deciding on what trick you want to teach, consider the availability of appropriate props. Using visually confusing items or those hard for the parrot to manipulate will result in failure. Browsing through toy departments, especially noting the kinds of toys available for toddlers and young children whose motor skills are not yet well developed, will give you some good ideas about what is available and could be worked into a trick for your bird. For example, large xylophones with colored metal keys and a stick for striking them may inspire you to develop Polly's musical talent!

A word about the safety and "parrot-proofing" props: Props must never be part of your bird's usual toy collection. Reserve them only for the trick they involve. Because of this, safety is not quite as critical. You would never place a bell in your parrot's cage with a clapper that could be easily dislodged and swallowed, or stuck in its beak or throat. However, you might use a large bell as a prop for a trick. If you do, a cow bell is advisable because it is large and easily manipulated by the bird. The clappers in cow bells may contain some lead, but as the bell will be used only for a particular trick, performed under the owner's close supervision, the metal content of the clapper should not be a threat. Flimsy props that will not stand up to the wear and tear of a parrot's beak and claws, or those that are obviously dangerous, should be avoided.

Readers who enjoy extraordinary success teaching their parrots simple tricks may want to progress to something more showy and dramatic. Roller skates and miniature scooters can be found through advertisements in various bird magazines.

The Basics of Trick Training

- Trick training is never coercive or punitive. Desired behavior is praised. Failure to perform correctly is ignored.

- Training sessions should be carried out daily, preferably at the same time.

- Food rewards should not constitute part of the parrot's daily diet, but be used only during training.

- The parrot should never be starved in order to increase its motivation to perform correctly for its food reward; however, if the parrot is slightly hungry, this will not impair its health and well-being and will increase the chance of learning success.

- The training area must be quiet and distraction-free.

- Food rewards and props should be at the training area before the parrot is brought there.

- Patience, patience, and more patience is required on the owner's part.

- The owner must have mentally worked out the trick to be taught in full, step by step, before the first session.

- Length of training sessions should not be less than ten minutes, but longer sessions should be determined by the bird's eagerness and attention span, neither of which should be exceeded.

- Training sessions should be fun for both owner and parrot and should end before the parrot becomes tired and bored.

- Train the trick step by step, in logical progression.

- Always reward a correct response, and never reward an incorrect one.

- Do not go on to a further step until the previous step has been completely mastered by the parrot.

- Always start trick training with simple, easily learned behaviors; save more complicated tricks for later.

- Never attempt a training session if you think your parrot is not feeling well. Contact your avian veterinarian and postpone training until the bird has a clean bill of health.

- If you don't feel well, or have had a really bad day that makes you cringe at the thought of a training session, omit the session for that day. Your parrot will pick up on your negative mood and will not work well. However, do not let this become an excuse for erratic training sessions.

- Trick training does not proceed in a smooth, continuous line. During one session your parrot may learn brilliantly, only to behave during the next session as if it has no clue why it's there or what you want of it. Be prepared for this, and don't allow it to spoil the fun of the session.

Designing a Trick for Your Parrot

It is evident from the above list that trick training can be a rather involved process. Or at least, it may seem so. But if you take the time to design a trick properly, step by logical step, your parrot should be able to learn at least simple behaviors and may become a real performing demon.

One thing is certain: If you are not perfectly clear about the steps needed for your parrot to learn a trick, your parrot never will be either.

So let's follow a simple trick, step by step. Once you have gone through this process, you can adapt it to any trick your parrot is mentally and physically capable of learning.

The first principle is to choose a behavior your parrot can learn, given careful, patient, repetitive training. It is possible, for instance, for most parrots to learn to shake "hands." By contrast, it is very unlikely that your parrot will ever be able to learn to fly through a flaming hoop. Some very talented parrots, with very experienced trainers, may learn such a behavior, but it is certainly nothing most of us would or should try.

The second principle is to start simple. After your parrot has mastered a number of simple tricks, you can progress to more involved ones.

The third principle is to be realistic about the time you have to commit to trick training. By definition, operant conditioning requires daily, repetitive work. Most of us can find the time, given sufficient motivation, to train simple tricks. But more involved ones, such as riding a bike or using skates, require too much time for most of us. It is far better to spend your available time on teaching a simple trick your parrot can learn successfully in a relatively short time than to attempt an impossible goal and fail. This gives a very negative message to the parrot and defeats the purpose of trick training.

Now, for the step-by-step plan for the trick. This example uses putting rings on a spindle.

First, obtain the necessary props. These will consist of a spindle and several rings with holes big enough to fit easily over it. You can purchase such a child's toy. However, many of these have a spindle set into a curved base that rocks back and forth. This is fine for a human toddler, but for a parrot, the base will have to be modified so it will sit firmly without moving. If you or another family member are handy, you can make your own spindle and purchase large wooden drapery rings to use with it. These can be left their natural color or brightly painted with nontoxic paint. An eight-inch spindle mounted on an eight-inch-by-eight-inch base will give the necessary stability and workability for medium to large parrots. For small parrots, a four-inch spindle with a smaller base will be best. Plastic shower curtain rings in bright colors can be used effectively.

Second, analyze very carefully the full range of activities your parrot will need to do in order to perform the trick correctly. Use paper and pencil to document the required motions. Then review the steps, noting anything you may have left out. Remember, your parrot will not know what the objects are or what they are to be used for at first. Nor does it have any idea what you want it to do. Your task is rather like explaining something to an extraterrestrial having no understanding of human artifacts, let alone human language.

Your list might look something like this:

- Show Polly props.

- Show Polly what to do with rings when I say, "Put rings on spindle." Do this several times. Perhaps use whole first session giving command and demonstrating trick. Bridge (praise) and "reward" myself by miming eating one of the cheese bits.

- Second session, demonstrate trick again several times, along with cue. Be sure to bridge and "reward" myself.

- Give cue and hand Polly ring.

- If Polly even touches ring, bridge and reward (give small piece of cheese).

- Spend whole second session rewarding for just touching ring.

- Third session, demonstrate trick with cue several times, bridging and "rewarding" myself, then give Polly cue and ring. This time, don't reward for just touching. Demonstrate trick with cue again, then give Polly cue and ring. If she doesn't perform, or just takes ring and drops it, ignore and demonstrate again.

- When the time arrives that Polly takes the ring and makes even a tentative move toward spindle, bridge and reward.

- Bridge and reward every time Polly takes ring and moves toward spindle, but between each attempt, remember to demonstrate using cue.

- Goal: to move Polly closer and closer to spindle when she has ring. Bridge and reward in later sessions only as she moves closer.

- At some point, Polly will perform trick correctly. Bridge and reward, then give her another ring with cue. Bridge and reward.

- Goal: to get Polly to put all the rings on the spindle before bridge and reward. To do this (after she is putting ring on the spindle routinely), withhold bridge and reward until second ring goes on the spindle. Slowly progress, giving bridge and reward after two rings on, then three, then four, then all five on spindle.

- Mission accomplished!

- Drill trick several times each day for a couple of weeks before starting to train a new trick. Remember always to bridge and reward.

- Have Polly do her trick away from the training area, for other family members. They're not going to believe this!

As you are making your list, see it from your parrot's view, as well as your own. The parrot's view might go something like this:

- Look at doughnut things on stick.

- Watch Beth take doughnut things off stick.

- Hear Beth say, "Put ring on spindle" (whatever *that* means!).

- Watch Beth put doughnut things, one by one, back on stick.

- Hear Beth say, "Put ring on spindle" and put those funny little doughnut things on that stick, many, *many* times! She seems awfully happy with herself, and she keeps eating!

- Hear Beth say, "Put ring on spindle" and see her give me a little doughnut thing (Do you suppose those things are called "rings"? [mental shrug]).

- Take ring thing and throw it on table.

- See Beth take ring thing, put on stick, saying "Put ring on spindle."

- See Beth hand me ring and say, "Put ring on spindle." I hold it in my beak instead of throwing it on the table. She says "Good bird!!" and gives me a tiny piece of cheese. Wonder what that was for? But it's good anyway, even if she was a little stingy.

- See Beth hand me ring again and say, "Put ring on spindle." I look away.

- See Beth hand me ring again and say, "Put ring on spindle." I take it and throw it down.

- Hear Beth say, "Put ring on spindle," and see her put ring on spindle. Hear Beth say, "Good girl, Beth!" See Beth eat a cheese bit. I don't get any. Cheese and ring go together?

- See Beth give me ring and say, "Put ring on spindle." I take ring and drop it close to spindle. Beth says "Good Polly! Good!" She gives me cheese. *Hmmmm* . . .

- See Beth give me ring and say, "Put ring on spindle." I take ring and drop it close to spindle. No cheese.

- Hear Beth say, "Put ring on spindle," then put ring on spindle herself. She says, "Good girl, Beth!" and eats more cheese. What's going on here?

- See Beth give me ring and say, "Put ring on spindle." I take ring and drop it over spindle. Beth goes nuts. She claps her hands and says, "Good girl, Polly! Good!" I get a piece of cheese. Maybe I'm getting somewhere, wherever *that's* supposed to be!

- Beth says, "Put ring on spindle," and hands me a ring. I drop it near spindle. Close, but no cheese.

- Beth says again, "Put ring on spindle," and hands me ring. I put ring on spindle. Beth says "Good girl, Polly." I get cheese!

- Beth says, "Put ring on spindle," and I pick one up from table and put it on spindle. Beth goes nuts again and tells me how good I am. Well, I really am exceptional. I get more love and cheese. I think I've figured this out. I find another ring and drop it on spindle. More cheese. Great! Two more rings left. More cheese if I put the silly things on the spindle? I do. More cheese. Okay, I could do this all day!

- Beth takes rings off spindle. Goody, we get to do it again! Wait a minute—she's picking me up. She's taking me back to my play gym. Oh, no! What happened to rings and cheese? I hope this isn't the end of a beautiful game. I love cheese, and Beth is *sooo* happy. I twist around and peer at the rings. Beth says, "You're a smart, good girl, Polly. We'll do rings on spindle again tomorrow." She gives me a big kiss. Somehow, I think I'm going to get more rings and cheese pretty soon. Aren't I the clever one!

The Model/Rival technique lends itself rather nicely to tricks such as our example.

It is a good idea to allow your parrot to become familiar with props before training begins, especially if the parrot is timid and tends to be fearful of new things. Place the props where the bird can see them routinely for several days before training begins. However, props should not be given to the parrot as playthings.

Teaching Specific Tricks

The following instructions are for teaching your parrot a few simple tricks. When choosing any of these tricks (or any you may devise yourself), take into account your parrot's personality and tolerance limits. For example, if your bird dislikes being touched on its back, it is probably not a good idea to try to teach it to roll over—unless you are deliberately trying to desensitize the parrot to being touched in this area. Even so, there are other less threatening and invasive ways of doing this, and they should be used. (See My *Parrot, My Friend* for an in-depth discussion of behavioral modification.) Tricks should be taught only for fun—both yours and the bird's—and to channel the parrot's physical and emotional energy.

If your parrot tends to be aggressive, boisterous, and unpredictable, do not teach it to give you a kiss. Sooner or later, particularly if the parrot is mature and is in breeding condition, you will be rewarded with a nasty nip. This trick should be taught only to a parrot that is extremely gentle and steady, and whose behavior is entirely predictable. I feel that Amazon parrots should never, under any circumstance, be allowed around one's face except in the most controlled or exceptional cases. Cockatoos, some macaws, and African Greys are probably the best candidates for this trick, because of their personalities. However, each bird is different, so use your best judgment and do not rely on species tendencies to determine whether teaching your parrot to kiss is a wise idea.

If your parrot is threatened by movements close to its face and reacts by lunging or attempting to bite, then trying to teach it to nod "yes" or shake its head "no" should not be attempted.

Some parrots are extremely sensitive about having their wings touched, so teaching it to be an "eagle" may not be a good idea. Ditto with parrots that loathe having their feet touched: Endeavoring to teach one to shake hands or wave should not be attempted until the bird is more comfortable with such contact.

Start with simple, easily learned tricks that give your parrot a good chance for a positive, successful experience on which future, more complicated behaviors can be built.

The instructions given below for various tricks are given step by step. The reader should understand that these instructions follow a logical course that may take many days or weeks—possibly even months—to complete. They cannot be accomplished in one or two sessions.

During any given session, the parrot may appear to have forgotten everything it learned in the previous sessions. This is not at all uncommon; in fact, it should be expected. When this happens, backtrack and review previous steps for as long as required. Demonstrate again as many times as necessary to refresh your parrot's memory and reinforce what it is supposed to be learning.

Always be alert to signs of flagging attention, frustration, or boredom, and take steps to correct the situation. Many times, merely picking the parrot up and walking around the room talking with it will provide enough of a break to allow the bird to work with enthusiasm again. If the end of the session is very near, you may want to break it off at this time, praising your parrot for the good job it did and returning it to its cage or play area.

The Kiss

Goal: The parrot gives a kiss whenever the cue is given.

This trick requires no props. Choose a small, easily grasped food reward. Choose the cue: "Gimme a kiss," or something similar. As with all tricks, teach this one in the selected training area. Determine the length of the training session. It can be extended based on your parrot's response. However, start with ten or fifteen minutes at first, then take it from there. Under no circumstances should you train this trick if you are ill, or even feeling a little under the weather. You don't want to pass germs to your bird. After the parrot has mastered the trick, it can be done away from the training area as you desire.

- Prepare the training area, with the food reward at hand.

- Set a timer for the length of the session. If your parrot shows signs of boredom or wandering attention, end the session happily, but early.

- Take the parrot to the training area and seat yourself, with the bird on your hand or arm, in a comfortable position.

- Place the reward between your lips.

- Raise the parrot so it can reach your mouth comfortably.

- Give the cue, "Gimme a kiss," and lean forward a bit so your parrot can see the food between your lips.

"Gimme a kiss."

- When the parrot leans forward to take the treat, allow it to have it, and bridge (praise).

- Continue training sessions, practicing until your parrot performs this behavior with confidence and without hesitation every time the cue is given.

- Once your parrot has thoroughly mastered the trick, omit the food reward from your lips and give it to the parrot with the bridge, immediately after it has touched your lips with its beak.

- Continue drilling the trick several times a day for one or two weeks before beginning to train another trick.

- When beginning to train a different trick, start each session by running through the kiss, and any other tricks your parrot has learned, before proceeding to the lesson at hand. This will start the session on a positive note and put your bird in the mood to learn something new.

Note: If you are uncomfortable beginning training this trick with the food reward between your lips, keep the reward in your hand and place your hand near your face. As training progresses, the reward can be moved closer to your mouth until it is, for all practical purposes, between your lips.

Shaking Hands

Goal: The parrot shakes "hands" whenever the cue is given.

No props are needed for this trick, other than a T-stand and food rewards.

- Prepare the training area with a T-stand; have the food reward ready.

- Set a timer for the length of the session. Be aware of your parrot's interest level and, if necessary, end the session early, but on a positive note.

- Take the parrot to the training area and place on the T-stand.

Hand shake.

- Review any tricks previously learned, then go on to shaking hands.

- Give the cue, "Shake," and touch the parrot's foot. When the foot is lifted, bridge (praise) and reward (feed).

- When the parrot is raising its foot consistently when given the cue, grasp its foot and shake it. Bridge and reward.

- When the last step has been accomplished, bridge and reward only after handshake (footshake!) has been properly completed. At this point, do not reward for merely lifting the foot.

- Continue drilling the trick daily, until your parrot performs on cue no matter where it is.

Note: Instead of the above, you may wish to give the cue and immediately grasp the parrot's foot and shake it, bridging and rewarding when the behavior has been successfully completed. This may confuse the parrot, however, as it may think you are trying to take it on your hand or arm. Your choice of methods for this trick depends on your parrot and how you think it will react to one method or the other.

The wave.

Waving

Goal: The parrot waves whenever the cue is given.

No props are needed other than a T-stand and food rewards.

- Choose the word you will use for cue: "Hello," "Bye-bye," or "Wave."

- Have the T-stand and food rewards ready in the training area.

- Set the timer for session length.

- Take the parrot to the training area and place on the T-stand.

- Review all tricks learned previously, then go on to the wave.

- Extend your finger and touch the parrot's foot, giving the cue.

- When the parrot raises its foot slightly, bridge (praise) and reward.

- When the parrot consistently raises its foot on cue, you must begin to encourage it to open and close its toes in an imitation of waving. To do this, you may gently stroke the bottom of its foot, which will cause the parrot to wiggle its toes in response. When this occurs, bridge and reward. Alternatively, you may wave your hand or fingers at the bird. When it begins to imitate this motion with its toes, bridge and reward.

- Continue to drill the trick until your parrot performs correctly every time the cue is given. At this point, back away from the bird when you give the cue. Continue to widen the space between you and the parrot until it performs the action on cue no matter where you are in the room.

- Practice the wave away from the training area after it has been mastered there.

Turn Around

Goal: The parrot turns 360 degrees whenever the cue "Turn around" is given.

No props are necessary for this trick other than a T-stand and food rewards.

Turn around.

- Prepare the training area with the T-stand and food rewards.

- Set the timer for session length.

- Take the parrot to the training area and place on the T-stand.

- Review previously learned tricks, then begin "turn around."

- With the parrot on the T-stand and the food reward in your hand, give the cue, "Turn around." As you do this, slowly circle your hand with the reward around the parrot's head, beginning in front, proceeding around the back, and ending up with your hand and the food in front of the parrot again.

- At first, bridge (praise) and reward (feed) if the parrot only turns its head slightly in the direction of your hand.

- When the parrot follows your hand around further, bridge and reward only for this.

- Eventually, the parrot will have to turn completely around on the perch to follow your hand further. When this happens, bridge and reward for this and nothing else.

- At this point, the parrot will be facing away from you. With food in hand, continue your hand movement until the parrot is again forced to turn all the way around, once again facing you, in order to get its praise and reward.

- When the parrot arrives at the point where it is turning a full 360 degrees on cue for praise and reward, continue drilling until the behavior is performed correctly whenever the cue is given.

- At this point, begin giving only the cue, without the accompanying hand movement. Bridge and reward only when the parrot performs correctly without the hand movement.

- Continue drilling the trick at every session until the parrot performs correctly with consistency.

- Practice the trick away from the training area, so your parrot will perform correctly no matter where it is.

Nodding "Yes"

Goal: The parrot nods "yes" whenever the cue is given.

No props are needed for this trick other than a T-stand and food rewards. The trick has more appeal for observers if the parrot is trained to nod "yes" to a specific question. After the trick has been mastered using one cue, another can be used to train it again. In this way, the parrot will build a repertoire of responses to various engaging questions. If you do this, train other tricks in between, so as not to confuse the bird. You must also review the trick with previous cues used before starting to teach the response with a different cue.

Nodding head "Yes."

- Pick the cue to be used: "Are you good bird?" "Are you bad bird?" "Love Mom (Dad)?" or "Nod yes."

- Prepare the training area with the T-stand and food rewards.

- Set the timer for session length.

- Take the parrot to the training area and place on the T-stand.

- Review previously learned tricks, remembering to bridge and reward.

- After review, face the parrot and give the cue, while at the same time moving your hand with the food reward up and down in front of the bird's face.

- When the parrot moves its head up and down to follow your hand motion, bridge (praise) and reward (feed).

- Continue drilling until the parrot nods "yes" whenever the cue is given.

- At this point, give the cue but withhold the hand motion. Bridge and reward only when the correct response is given.

- Continue practicing until the parrot gives the proper response without hesitation, even though you are no longer using your hand for it to follow.

- When your parrot is "picture perfect" with this trick in the training area, begin to practice away from there until it gives the proper response on cue no matter where it is.

Shaking Head "No"

Goal: The parrot shakes its head "No" whenever it is given the cue.

No props are needed for this trick other than a T-stand and food rewards. Again, this trick is more amusing if the parrot is trained to shake its head "No" in response to a cue that has some meaning, such as "Are you bad bird?" "Like medicine?" or "Are you a stinker?" If you wish to train responses to multiple cues, train only one at a time and intersperse training alternate cues with other completely different tricks to avoid confusing the parrot.

Shaking head "No."

- Prepare the training area with the T-stand and food rewards.

- Set the timer for session length.

- Take the parrot to the training area and place on the T-stand.

- Review previously learned tricks, remembering to bridge and reward.

- Proceed exactly as for training nodding head "yes," using the cue you have chosen, *except* that the hand holding the reward will be moved back and forth in front of the parrot's face rather than up and down.

Dancing.

Dance

Goal: The parrot "dances" whenever the cue is given.

No props are needed for this trick other than a T-stand and food rewards. Once the parrot has mastered the basic trick, it can be spiced up a bit by playing some of its favorite music and giving the cue. Some parrots groove on rock and heavy metal; others prefer Bach minuets. J.B. loves Vivaldi's *The Four Seasons,* but Mac adored country and western. The choice is yours and your bird's!

- Prepare the training area with the T-stand and food rewards.

- Set the timer for session length.

- Take the parrot to the training area and place on the T-stand.

- Review previously learned tricks, remembering to bridge and reward.

- Facing the parrot, give the cue, "Let's dance," while holding the reward in your hand at arm's length.

- Sway completely from one end of the perch to the other.

- When the parrot begins to sway from one side to the other in imitation of your movements, bridge (praise) and reward (feed).

- Continue drilling until the parrot responds correctly and consistently whenever the cue is given.

- At this point, omit your own body movements, give the cue, and bridge and reward only when the parrot responds correctly.

- When the parrot has completely mastered the trick, you may add music to heighten the effect of dancing. If you do this, be sure to continue to practice without music, too, so the parrot understands that with or without music, the trick is to be performed whenever the verbal cue is given.

- Practice the trick in a variety of places, once it is being performed correctly every time in the training area.

Eagle

Goal: The parrot spreads its wings to their full extent whenever the cue is given.

No props are needed for this trick other than a T-stand and food rewards.

The eagle.

- Prepare the training area with the T-stand and food rewards.

- Set the timer for session length.

- Take the parrot to the training area and place on the T-stand.

- Review previously learned tricks, remembering to bridge and reward.

- Facing the parrot, give the cue, "Eagle," and gently place your hands under the bird's wings, lifting them up and out as far as it will permit.

- When the parrot begins to lift its wings, even a tiny bit, on cue, bridge (praise) and reward (feed).

- Continue working with the parrot until it extends its wings fully on cue. You will probably have to help the bird, bit by bit, using your hands under its wings, to reach this point.

- The first time the parrot fully extends its wings using only the verbal cue, bridge and reward. Do not bridge and reward for less than fully extended wings without any help from this point on.

- Continue drilling the trick until the parrot has fully mastered it.

- When the trick has been fully mastered in the training area, begin to practice it outside this area until the parrot performs correctly wherever it is upon hearing the cue.

Note: Teaching your parrot a trick is not an exact science, as you probably realize by now. Sometimes it is necessary to modify the basic instructions in order to make it clearer to the parrot what is expected of it. One Blue and Gold Macaw apparently felt that merely lifting its wings a fraction from its body constituted doing an "eagle." Finally, its owner, in frustration, began giving the cue and spreading her own arms out as far as they would go in order to demonstrate what she wanted her parrot to do. It worked!

High Five (High Four!)

Goal: The parrot gives the owner a "high five" whenever the cue is given.

No props are needed for this trick, other than a T-stand and food rewards.

- Prepare the training area with the T-stand and food rewards.

- Set the timer for session length.

- Take the parrot to the training area and review previously learned tricks.

- Facing the parrot, give the cue, "Gimme five (or four)," and extend your finger to touch the parrot's foot.

- When the parrot lifts its foot in response to your finger touch, bridge (praise) and reward (feed).

- Continue to work with the parrot, encouraging it to raise its foot higher and higher, until you can place the tips of your fingers on the bottom of its foot. As it progresses, bridge and reward only for the most recent, best efforts, not beginning efforts.

- When the parrot has successfully mastered the trick in the training area, practice it in other locations.

Coins in the Bank

Goal: The parrot will place a given number of coins in a piggy bank whenever it is given the cue.

Coins in the bank.

In addition to the T-stand (for reviewing previously learned tricks not requiring props), you will need a suitable table, a piggy bank, coins or poker chips, and food rewards. If you use coins, they should be no smaller than a quarter. Because money is literally filthy lucre, put the coins in a cloth bag (or wrapped securely in cheesecloth so they don't fly all over the dishwasher and wreak havoc with the pump) or the covered receptacle in the silverware holder of the dishwasher and run them through a cycle. If you do not have a dishwasher, scrub the coins vigorously, then allow them to soak for five or six hours in a solution of Wavecide™, following the manufacturer's directions for dilution. After disinfecting, rinse thoroughly.

The piggy bank should be large and sturdy, with an opening to allow retrieval of the coins. The slot should be large enough to allow the parrot to insert the coins without undue frustration.

- Set up the training area with the T-stand, table, bank, coins, and food rewards.

- Set the timer for session length.

- Take the parrot to the training area and place on the T-stand.

- Review all previously learned tricks, remembering to bridge and reward.

- Place the parrot on the table (or alternatively, allow it to remain on the T-stand) and demonstrate placement of the coins in the bank, giving yourself the cue, "Go to the bank." After each demonstration, bridge and "reward" yourself.

- When you feel the trick has been adequately demonstrated, place the parrot on the table, hand it a coin, and give the cue.

- At first, bridge (praise) and reward (feed) whenever your parrot takes the coin from your hand.

- The first time the parrot begins to move toward the piggy bank, bridge and reward. From now on, bridge only for movement toward the bank with a coin.

- Work on getting the parrot ever closer to the bank, bridging and rewarding for the most recent, improved performance and not for lesser efforts.

- When your parrot attempts to place the coin in the slot, bridge and reward, and ignore any attempts that do not go this far.

- Your parrot may need a little help at first to get the coin into the slot successfully. This is okay. Bridge and reward for this behavior until the bird begins to succeed at actually getting the coin in without help. After this happens, bridge and reward only for this.

- When your parrot has mastered placement of one coin in the bank, work on placement of all the coins. (No more than four or five coins are recommended for this trick.) Do this by placing the first coin, along with the second, on the table and giving the verbal cue while handing the bird one coin at a time. The third, fourth, and fifth coins are trained in the same way.

- After the parrot has mastered placing all the coins in the bank, begin to omit handing the coins to it and start instead pointing at each coin while giving the verbal cue.

- When the trick has been mastered with finger pointing and the verbal cue, begin to eliminate pointing at the coins, giving only the verbal cue. Eventually, the parrot should be able to place all the coins in the bank with only the initial verbal cue.

- After the trick has been mastered in the training area, practice it in other locations.

Rings on the Spindle

Goal: The parrot places a completed set of rings on a spindle whenever the cue is given.

For this trick, you will need a table and a set of colored rings on a spindle. These are usually graduated in size unless you have made your own set. (See the section on prop suggestions for this trick.)

This is the first really complex trick you will teach your parrot. The parrot will be learning this behavior sequentially. In other words, the rings will be placed on the spindle in a specific order, depending upon their size. So not only must your parrot learn to do this correctly, it must first grasp the concept of placing a ring on the spindle—any ring—before it can go on to "bigger things." It may take many weeks before complete mastery occurs, so be patient. And keep training sessions fun for you both!

- Prepare the training area with a suitable table, props, and food rewards. Include the T-stand for review of previously learned tricks.

- Set the timer for length of session.

- Take the parrot to the training area and place on the T-stand.

- Review previously learned tricks, remembering to bridge and reward.

Rings on the spindle.

- Allow the parrot to remain on the T-stand, and demonstrate placing all the colored rings on the empty spindle. Remember to give the cue, "Put rings on spindle," before each demonstration. Praise and "reward" yourself.

- Spend the entire first session demonstrating the trick.

- During the second session, you may begin "hands-on" work with your parrot.

- Place the parrot on the table with the rings and empty spindle.

- Hand the parrot one of the rings (the largest, if you are using a set of graduated sizes) and give the cue.

- Bridge (praise) and reward (feed) when the parrot first takes the ring from your hand.

- Continue to bridge and reward up to the time the parrot first begins to move toward the spindle with the ring in its beak. When this point is reached, bridge and reward only when the parrot does this, not if it merely takes the ring in its beak.

- Continue to work at getting the parrot to move closer to the spindle with the ring. When it first makes the attempt to place the ring on the spindle, helping a little by moving the spindle closer to the bird is allowed. When the parrot gets to this point, bridge and reward; cease bridging and rewarding for anything less.

- Once it is consistently placing the ring correctly, begin to eliminate handing the ring to the parrot and begin to point at it when giving the cue.

- When the parrot is consistently placing one ring properly on cue, and with signal only, point to the second ring and give the cue again.

- Continue working until the parrot can put the entire set of rings on the spindle with just one cue, given at the beginning of the trick. If the rings are graduated in size, always encourage the bird to place them on the spindle in correct order.

- Gradually omit pointing to the rings, until the parrot can perform the trick with only the verbal cue.

- When the parrot has successfully mastered this trick in the training area, practice it elsewhere.

Putting Together a Simple Puzzle

Goal: The parrot correctly places all parts of a simple puzzle.

In addition to a T-stand, for review of previously learned tricks, you will need to equip the training area with a suitable table, the puzzle to be used, and food rewards. If other tricks involving props have been learned, include these for review, as well.

The puzzle should be extremely simple, with no more than four

Putting together a simple puzzle.

large, colorful pieces. Puzzles having one square, one circle, one triangle, and one oblong are best. Wooden puzzles of this type are highly recommended and are available wherever furnishings and learning toys for early childhood are sold. Place a large cup screw in each puzzle piece so your parrot will be able to grasp and manipulate it with ease.

This trick, like placing graduated rings on a spindle, is taught and learned sequentially. The parrot is taught to place one piece at a time correctly, until it is able to place all the pieces correctly with only one initial verbal cue. When first teaching puzzle piece placement, handing each piece to the bird is necessary. As the parrot approaches mastery, handing the pieces is replaced by a pointing finger. Eventually, the pointing is eliminated and only the verbal cue is given.

This trick is complex. Not only must the parrot recognize the piece, but it must manipulate it into correct position in the puzzle bed. And it must do this with three, or even four, pieces. Be prepared to spend many weeks teaching this trick, but don't become discouraged if progress seems slow. Remember that the object of trick training is to channel mental and emotional energy and provide structured, enjoyable time with you for your bird. It's the *process* that is the most important thing. Mastery of the trick is the secondary goal, the icing on the cake!

- Prepare the training area with the T-stand, table, puzzle, and food rewards.

- Set the timer for session length.

- Take the parrot to the training area and place it on the T-stand.

- Review previously learned tricks.

- After review, remove all props but the puzzle to be used.

- Demonstrate placement of the first puzzle piece, giving the cue, "Do puzzle." Bridge and "reward" yourself.

- After you feel the trick has been demonstrated adequately, give the cue and hand your parrot the puzzle piece.

- When your parrot takes the piece, bridge (praise) and reward (feed).

- Work on getting the parrot to move toward the puzzle base, eventually rewarding only for definite movement toward the base with the puzzle piece.

- When your parrot first attempts to place the puzzle piece correctly, bridge and reward. Later, bridge and reward for nothing less than solid proficiency.

- Continue to work with your parrot until it can place the puzzle piece into the base with the correct orientation. Once the parrot has achieved this, do not bridge and reward for incorrect placement.

- Continue to work with the first puzzle piece until your parrot has mastered its placement.

- When the parrot has mastered the trick with the verbal cue and being handed the puzzle piece, begin to point at the piece rather than handing it to the bird.

- Bridge and reward when the parrot picks up the piece without being handed it and places it correctly into the puzzle base.

- When your parrot has successfully mastered placement of the piece with pointed finger and verbal cue, place the first piece on the table, along with the second piece.

- After the parrot has successfully placed the first piece, demonstrate the proper placement of the second piece as many times as you feel necessary.

- Point to the second piece and give the verbal cue. When your parrot takes the second piece, bridge and reward.

- Proceed with training placement of the second piece as you did for the first.

- After correct placement of the first and second puzzle pieces has been mastered, proceed to the third. Work as you did with the second piece, having the parrot correctly place the first two pieces, then going on to the third.

- If your puzzle has a fourth piece, train its placement as above.

- After the parrot has mastered placement of all puzzle pieces correctly, begin practicing outside the training area.

Play Dead

Goal: The parrot plays "dead" whenever it is given the cue.

This trick requires no props. It should be taught over a soft surface, in case the parrot falls. The training area should be prepared with a T-stand, table, and props for reviewing previously learned tricks, as well as food rewards.

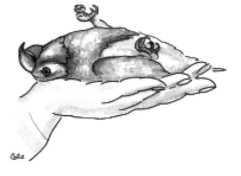

Play dead.

Most parrots dislike being on their backs at first, so this trick should be approached with patience and gentleness. It usually takes a great deal of time for the bird to become accustomed to and comfortable with this posture, as in the wild—or for pets experiencing tremendous stress and fear—it signifies the last line of defense before surrender and death. For this reason, if your parrot is naturally fearful and timid, omit this trick from the bird's repertoire. Reserve it for the boisterous, self-confident extrovert that likes lots of physical contact with you.

- Prepare the training area with the T-stand, food rewards, and a suitably soft surface. This can be a double bed, a carpeted floor, or an exercise mat.

- Set the timer for session length.

- Take the parrot to the training area and place on the T-stand.

- Review previously learned tricks, then move to the table to review those behaviors involving props. Always remember to bridge and reward.

- After the review is completed, take the parrot to the soft surface and position yourself comfortably with the bird on your hand or arm.

- If your parrot is not used to being touched on its back, you will need to acclimate it. Begin by resting your hand gently on its back for as long as the bird will tolerate it. Continue to do this, working up to progressively longer tolerance time. Do not proceed with teaching the parrot to play dead until it is completely at ease with having your hand on its back for at least a minute or two.

- The next step is to accustom the parrot to having its body encompassed by your hands. Do this by putting the parrot on the training surface and placing one hand on its back and the other clasping its chest gently. Take as long as is required for the bird to accept this comfortably. Do not proceed to the next step until this has been accomplished.

- When your bird is entirely comfortable with having its body encircled by your hands, give the cue, "Play dead," and tilt it very slightly backward. Gently return the parrot to an upright position and bridge (praise) and reward (feed).

- If your parrot loses its sense of equilibrium, struggles, or attempts to nip in fright, set it upright immediately and calm it. You must use your own best judgment about how soon to repeat the maneuver.

- Continue to work with the parrot to get it to accept more tilting, until it is comfortable in a reclining position. Bridge and reward for each maneuver (after returning the parrot to an upright position). As with other tricks, as the parrot becomes more tolerant of a position closer to a full recline, omit bridging and rewarding for lesser efforts.

- The goal of all the foregoing is to have the parrot lie flat on its back in the palm of your hand.

- When your parrot has mastered lying on its back in your hand, work to increase the time it remains in this position. Ten or fifteen seconds is fine. If, however, your parrot wants to lie there longer, good for it and for you!

- At this point, with the parrot lying in your hand, gently press its head backward a bit, to give the impression of a limp, lifeless body, while repeating the cue. Bridge and reward.

- When your parrot has completely mastered this behavior, including hanging its head down while it is on its back in your hand, you are ready to begin practicing away from the training area.

Roll Over

Goal: The parrot rolls over whenever the cue is given.

No props are needed for this trick. However, the training area should be equipped with food rewards, table and props, and T-stand for reviewing previously learned tricks at the beginning of each session. You will also need a soft surface: a bed, carpet, or exercise mat.

Ideally, this trick should be taught after the parrot has learned to play dead. The parrot must be comfortable with having its body encircled by your hands and being placed on its back.

Roll over.

As with "Play dead," do not attempt to teach a shy, timid, or fearful bird, or one that does not tolerate handling well, this trick. If this is the case, and you feel the bird would eventually be a candidate for this trick, begin with "Play Dead," accustoming the parrot gently and patiently over time to accept a full body grasp. Go at the parrot's pace and level of tolerance, and do not hesitate to backtrack if the bird exhibits fear or lack of tolerance at progressively encompassing handling.

This trick, as the previous one, will take a long time for the parrot to master. Do not exceed its tolerance level, and always use patience and gentleness when working with your bird on this, or any, trick.

- Prepare the training area with needed items.

- Set the timer for session length.

- Take the parrot to the training area and review previously learned tricks.

- When you feel your bird is comfortable with a full body embrace and being on its back, it is ready to start learning to roll over.

- Take the parrot to the soft surface and sit down with it, allowing it to stand on the surface.

- Encircle the parrot's body with your hands and place it gently on its back. Give the cue, "Roll over," and roll the parrot onto its side, bridging (praising) and rewarding (feeding) as soon as you complete this maneuver.

- When your parrot is completely comfortable with being placed on its back and rolled on its side, proceed to the next phase.

- Place the parrot on its back, give the cue, and roll it on its side, then continue by rolling it on its tummy. Bridge and reward.

- When the parrot is completely comfortable with the above activity, continue the rolling motion from side to tummy to its other side.

- The next step is to complete the rolling movement, with the parrot on its back once again. Bridge and reward for only the latest phase of the rolling maneuver.

- When the parrot is comfortable with the entire rolling-over exercise, begin to give only the verbal cue, omitting the "hands-on" aspect. You may have to help with a little nudge the first few times, but omit this as soon as possible. As with other training, bridge and reward for only the desired behavior once the parrot demonstrates that it understands and can perform the particular step you want.

- When your parrot has mastered this trick using only the verbal cue, you are ready to begin doing the trick away from the training area.

Choosing the Correct Color

Goal: The parrot will choose the correct color on cue, when presented with a limited number of choices.

This behavior can be taught using the Model/Rival technique of speech training. When

Choosing the correct color.

utilizing this method, you are working to enlarge the parrot's intellectual and speech capacity—teaching it not only to recognize the color, but to associate it with the word symbol for that color and use it appropriately. However, the method given here does not aim for these goals, but merely teaches the parrot to recognize the right color and choose it from a variety of other color choices.

In addition to food rewards and the equipment you routinely used for previously learned tricks, you will need to equip the training area with a table, as well as the colored objects needed for the trick. Be sure these objects can be easily grasped by the parrot's beak. If not, affix cup hooks to facilitate this.

The use of only four colors is recommended at first: blue, green, yellow, and red. After the parrot has mastered these colors, you may add others, if you wish. You may also change the objects bearing the colors the bird has already learned. For example, if the parrot was trained in color recognition using a set of child's stacking cups, you might want to substitute keys of the same color, or small building blocks painted with nontoxic paint.

This trick is learned sequentially, as with putting rings on a spindle or correctly placing puzzle pieces. It would be helpful to review the teaching instructions for these tricks before starting to train color recognition.

This is a complex trick, and it may take quite some time for your parrot to master it.

- Prepare the training area with food rewards, T-stand, table, props used for trick review, and the color objects to be used for this trick.

- Set the timer for session length.

- Take the parrot to the training area and review previously learned tricks.

- Begin teaching this trick using one of the colored objects. For the purpose of this set of instructions, we will assume the use of red, blue, green, and yellow child's stacking cups with a hook in the bottom to allow your parrot to grasp the cup easily.

- Give yourself the cue, "Pick out red," and pick up the red cup. Bridge and "reward" yourself.

- Demonstrate this several times, always using the same color. You may want to spend the whole first session demonstrating.

- Place your parrot on the table, with the red cup eight to twelve inches away from the bird.

- Give the cue, and when the parrot moves toward the cup, bridge (praise) and reward (feed).

- Work with the parrot to get it to move closer and closer to the red cup. Every time it moves closer, bridge and reward, and cease bridging and rewarding for lesser efforts.

- When the parrot finally picks up the red cup, bridge and reward. From this time, do this only when the parrot moves to, and picks up, the red cup.

- Work with the parrot until it has mastered picking up the red cup, then place the cup twice the distance from its original position in relation to the bird.

- Continue drilling this behavior until the parrot will retrieve the red cup from anyplace on the table.

- When the parrot has mastered "long-distance" retrieval, place the red and green cups side by side on the table, about eight to twelve inches from the bird.

- Pick up the green cup, giving yourself the cue, "Pick out green." Bridge and "reward" yourself. Demonstrate this several times.

- Next, give yourself the cue, "Pick out red," and pick up the red cup. Bridge and "reward" yourself. Follow this with several more demonstrations with the green cup, giving yourself the cue, and bridging and "rewarding" yourself. Repeat this sequence several times, one "red cup" to five "green cups."

- Place the parrot on the table and give the cue, "Pick out green cup." If the parrot moves toward the green cup, bridge and reward. If, on the other hand, it makes a beeline for the red cup, ignore and repeat the cue, "Pick out green."

- Repeat this exercise until your parrot picks up the green cup consistently on cue.

- When the parrot has mastered the green cup, begin to alternate cues—first red, then green—until it can pick up either cup correctly on cue.

- As with working on the red cup alone, begin to move the cups farther and farther away from the parrot, working toward having it pick up whichever cup is requested from any position on the table.

- At this point, place the yellow cup next to the red and green cups, eight to twelve inches from the parrot. Demonstrate as you did when introducing the green cup.

- Proceed with training as you did when the second color was introduced. When the parrot has mastered red, green, and yellow cups correctly on cue, from anywhere on the table, add the blue cup and proceed in the same way as you did with each new color introduction.

- When the parrot has mastered all four colors from any position on the table in the training area, begin to practice in other locations.

- At this point, you may wish to substitute other objects of the same color and retrain the trick. You may be surprised how much more quickly the parrot learns the trick, having already learned to identify its colors.

- At some time, you may wish to train for more colors, such as pink, purple, orange, and black. Be sure that the colors are completely different, so the parrot is not confused by shades of the same color. As with the original colors trained, work with only four at a time.

What Has Been Learned in This Chapter?

- Teaching parrots tricks is a good way to channel mental and physical energy and provide positive experiences that result in appropriately given praise and attention.

- The time parrot and owner spend together in trick training sessions contributes positively to their strong bonding.

- Teaching a parrot tricks uses operant conditioning, in which the parrot performs a behavior correctly for a reward.

- Operant conditioning requires the use of a cue (command), a bridge (praise when the behavior is correctly performed), and a reward (food).

- Although some parrots will perform for praise only, appropriate food rewards, consisting of small bits of healthy food, are the most effective training rewards.

- Although the parrot must never be starved in order to motivate it to learn and perform, a parrot that is slightly hungry will usually work harder and learn more quickly to obtain the coveted treat.

- Training sessions should take place no less often than once daily if any real progress is to be made. Sessions should last a minimum of ten to fifteen minutes. Some parrots will remain interested and attentive for longer periods, but in no case should the session last so long the parrot becomes "turned off" and begins to view trick training as a negative experience.

- Trick training *never* involves the use of punishment of any kind.

- Tremendous patience is needed when teaching your parrot a trick, because—depending upon the trick being taught—it may take days, weeks, or even months for the parrot to master a given behavior.

- If the parrot, after dedicated, patient training for a period of time, does not seem to be able to master a trick, it is best to drop that particular trick and go on to another better suited to that parrot's interest and ability, rather than let the bird develop a negative attitude about trick training in general.

- The tricks you teach your bird should be selected with a view to the parrot's personality and tolerance level; otherwise your efforts may well be doomed to failure. Do not attempt to train tricks for which your parrot is temperamentally unsuited.

- Before you start teaching a trick, design it carefully to include every step the parrot will have to master in order to perform the completed behavior. Be sure to look at your plan from the parrot's standpoint, as well, because this will help you avoid potential confusion and increase the parrot's chances of success.

- The owner must have a good working knowledge of trick training basics before beginning to work with the parrot.

- In order for the parrot to enjoy its sessions and view them positively, the owner must be alert for signs of boredom, flagging attention, or frustration, and take steps to remedy the situation if it occurs.

- Trick training should be fun for both parrot and owner; otherwise the reason for doing it will be defeated.

- The training area should be quiet, distraction-free, and furnished with all necessary equipment and props before the parrot is brought to the area for a session.

11

Playing with Your Parrot

It is clever to play, but not to stop playing.

—Polish proverb

The saying quoted above is a wise one, for when we forget the joy and spontaneity of play in our relationships with our birds, we and they have lost much of the savor of living together. We humans often forget the place of fun in our lives as we become adults. However, parrots are among the few creatures that retain a sense of fun and play into adulthood. All young animals play as a way to practice and hone their future survival skills.

Parrots' continued play as adults seems to be for the sheer fun of it, because their antics and puckish sense of humor do not seem to have any survival value, but merely enhance their quality of life and general *joie de vivre*.

Parents of young children often recapture the fun of playing when they play with their children. People who share their lives with parrots can play with them, too. It can be just as much fun. Playing with your parrot should be spontaneous. Play sessions don't have to last long. Nor do they have to occur on a daily basis, unlike formal training sessions (although it's wonderful if they do). Short periods of play can be interspersed with other activities throughout the day. As with other activities we do with our parrots, playing together helps strengthen the human/parrot bond, provides quality interaction for the bird with its owner, and helps prevent boredom and the behavioral problems often seen in understimulated parrots.

A parrot's sense of play is somewhat different from ours. Although they certainly do like to play in an active, physical way, more passive activities we would not ordinarily classify as play may indeed be just that for our parrots. This is because parrots resemble in their understanding and intellectual levels two- to three-year-old human toddlers.

Cole

A.J. Cole in a playful, silly mood.

As with human toddlers, parrots tend to have relatively short attention spans. They are very self-centered creatures, much like the two- or three-year-old child, whose favorite words during this time are "Mine" and "No." Parrots, as is the case with young children, have very little ability to relate to the needs and wants of others. A parrot, just as a small child, will play intensely and boisterously with a favorite toy for a period, then suddenly abandon it when something else captures its attention. The same often occurs when the parrot is playing interactively with its owner. After a few minutes of enthusiastic participation, it may suddenly lose interest and turn its attention to something entirely different. In any given play encounter, your physical nearness may be as important as, or more important than, the activity itself. Too, parrots are very much like human toddlers in their sense of curiosity and mischief.

Soucek

Daisy, a Spectacled Amazon, enjoys a solo play session.

Passive Play and Interactive Play

As with young children, parrots can engage in both passive play and interactive play.

Passive play, when engaged in by young children, is also called parallel play. At times, passive play may be just the thing for you and your parrot. At others, both of you may want to engage in interactive play. For the owner, having the alternatives of passive and interactive play gives the choice of how you will spend play time with your parrot, depending on your own schedule and "to do" list, while at the same time sharing quality time with your parrot.

In passive play, the parrot (or youngster) will be engaged in its own activity in very close proximity to the owner (or parent, or another child), who is doing his or her "own thing." In this kind of play, the physical closeness, coupled with each individual doing whatever he or she wants to do, provides a lot of quiet satisfaction and a sense of security and togetherness for the parrot.

In interactive play, the twosome, whether it be parrot and owner or child and playmate, do things *with* each other instead of *alongside* each other.

Using Passive Play

As you have probably guessed by now, these two kinds of play can be used very satisfactorily to provide fun for your parrot while allowing you, the owner, the choice of activities. This can be a relief. Remember that what to you may not be play may be fascinating for your bird. Passive play often serves to meet both the parrot's needs and the owner's at the same time.

Soucek

**Piper, another of Gayle Soucek's parrots,
training for a career as a secretary.**

For example, say you are pressed for time and you must get the bills paid *tonight*. But you also want to play with your parrot and are feeling a bit guilty because Polly will have to hang out in her cage while you wrestle with the checkbook. If Polly is anything like our J.B., she will adore being placed on a perch near or on your desk and being given her own envelope to chew and destroy. For many parrots, watching paper and pen being used by their owners seems to provide a lot of fun and amusement. This is passive play. (Well, maybe not to the bill payer!) It allows the parrot to be a part of the activity while it observes—close up—its owner doing something interesting, at the same time having one of those intriguing pieces of paper to play with. It's a win-win situation, because the owner not only gets the bills paid, but he or she doesn't have to feel guilty for neglecting the parrot that particular evening.

The same scenario can be translated to any number of situations. Your parrot can have a seat on its T-stand next to the kitchen counter while you chop vegetables or mix cake or cookie batter. It's even better if Polly can sample a bit of what you're working with. Or perhaps you have a shower perch for your parrot. Many parrots love this, and the owner can go happily about morning ablutions in the company of his or her parrot while providing a fun start to the day for Polly.

Reading to your bird is a kind of passive play in that the parrot is close to you and can listen to your voice, enjoying your company as you enjoy both your bird and the story you're reading aloud. Watching television together is a similar example of passive play.

Another kind of passive play is taking your parrot—suitably confined in a carrier that allows it to observe the passing sights—for a drive in the car. You can do this just for the fun of it, or to include Polly while you run an errand or two.

If she is accompanying you on errands, you will need to observe a few precautions. Be sure the weather is not to too hot or cold, because Polly will have to wait in the car while you run into the dry cleaners or drop that book off at the library. Be sure to lock the car door in your absence—and make sure your absence from the car is *brief*. It is not safe or appropriate to take your bird on lengthy errands like the weekly shopping or a leisurely stroll through the hardware store. Last, don't take your parrot with you into whatever establishment your errands take you, even if the parrot is welcome there. The danger of losing your bird is too great should it become startled by passing traffic, someone walking a strange dog in the vicinity, or any number of circumstances that could cause it to jump in panic from your hand or arm. Even parrots with trimmed wing feathers have been known to take flight if a gust of wind comes along and provides enough lift for take-off. In this situation, the parrot may well be able to travel just far enough to make retrieval difficult or even impossible, not to mention the horrible possibility that it could fly into traffic.

Using Interactive Play

This includes all the play activities that require interaction between bird and owner.

One thing you might like to try with your parrot is coloring! Use a coloring book that appeals to you, and get a big box of nontoxic crayons (the kind your mother would never buy you because she said you didn't need all those colors!). Put your parrot alongside you on the table and see what happens. If Polly grabs your crayon, no harm done, as long as you don't allow her to consume the entire thing. You may be very surprised to find that both you and your bird thoroughly enjoy your "art" sessions.

You may wish to dance with your bird. Some parrots, especially the large macaws and cockatoos, enjoy this tremendously. Put on your favorite music, place Polly on your arm, and sashay around the floor. The drama of it all is often a big turn-on for socially inclined parrots.

Some parrots like being included in housework. Many years ago I had a large macaw that adored climbing down from his cage while I cleaned the floor. He was very nosy and constantly tried to snatch the whisk broom I used under the cages (before the Dust Buster era). I finally gave up and let him have the whisk broom. To my surprise, he actually attempted to sweep particles into the dust pan I was holding and actually got a bit into the pan. I was astounded! "Creb" wasn't a very efficient cleaner, but he enjoyed trying, and we both had a bit of fun.

You might like to get a set of children's large building blocks. Sit on the floor with your parrot and construct a block tower, then watch the bird knock it down. Just be sure you don't build the tower so high the blocks hit the bird on the head during its demolition project.

Birdie aerobics provide the opportunity for interactive play. With your parrot on your hand or arm, encourage it to flap its wings by moving your arm down and then up, in a large circle. Move slowly so as not to alarm the parrot or cause it to lose its balance and fall.

"Aerobics" could also include "walking" your parrot. Various avian supply companies sell parrot harnesses. These fit around the parrot's body in a manner similar to a cat harness. A leash is attached so you and your parrot can take a walk. Obviously, you will need to determine whether your parrot will tolerate and enjoy this kind of exercise. If so, you must take care that your walking route is safe for the bird. Remember that any surface, whether indoor flooring, grass, or concrete, is home to millions of germs. Remember also that parrots hold food in their feet and groom their feet with their tongues and beaks. This means that you need to be extremely careful of where you walk your parrot. I strongly recom-

Doane

Three of the author's parrots—J.B., Molly, and Mac—enjoy each other's company under "Mom's" supervision.

mend that if you do this, you thoroughly clean your bird's feet with a gentle disinfectant soap when you finish your walk together.

Another interactive game many parrots enjoy is playing peek-a-boo. There are many variations on this game. You can cover your face with your hands, then remove them and say the "magic words." You can peek around the door and say "peek-a-boo." You can cover the parrot's eyes with your hands and then remove them. Or you can cover its face with a hand towel or washcloth for the game. When using any of these variations, be sure your bird will not be frightened by them. Because there are so many ways to play the game, you should be able to settle on a variation that amuses rather than startles or frightens. One of my macaws was so taken with playing peek-a-boo that he began to play it by himself, covering one of his eyes with a foot, or holding a toy in front of his face, then jerking it away and screaming "peek-a-boo" as loudly as he was able!

Some parrots are into "playing ball." A soft foam ball can be used, as can a whiffle ball—the kind made for practicing indoor golf shots. A compactly wadded piece of paper will also work. While your parrot is on its cage or play gym, or on the sofa with you, gently toss the ball and let the bird retrieve it. Many birds prefer to chew on the ball, but quite a few will learn to toss it back with encouragement from their owners. Pam Willis's Blue-fronted Amazon, Tiko, is a real master at this game.

A variation on playing ball is letting your parrot toss a toy onto the floor, from whence you, the lucky owner, get to retrieve it and hand it back. I have never yet met a parrot that didn't play this game with enthusiasm. Perhaps it gives them a sense of power to see their owners groveling about the floor at the parrot's whim!

Many parrots love to have their owners call to them from another room. This kind of antiphonal vocalization mimics the calling of one parrot to another in the wild as they forage apart from flock or mate. Some parrots even learn new words this way. The macaw who so enjoyed playing peek-a-boo did this. He called out a word, and I responded with another. Pretty soon, he was saying the second word!

Playing tag is another game that some parrots like. Do this with your parrot only if it is a happy, self-confident little guy. Mac, my Timneh Grey, loved to be placed on the bed. I would then say, "I'm gonna get you!" He would commence to bounce around the bed in mock terror as I pursued him and gently grasped his tail feathers and gave them a little waggle. I got tired of the game long before he did—every time.

A bit of fun and whimsy lowers the blood pressure, lightens the daily routine, and rests the mind. It appeals to the child in us and the children that are our parrots. Use your imagination and add a little playtime to your and your parrot's life. You'll be glad you did!

What Has Been Learned in This Chapter?

- Play is fun; playing with our parrots is not a chore, but a spontaneous, joyful way to be together.

- Parrots, unlike most animals other than primates, whales, and dolphins, play throughout their lives.

- Parrots are similar to human preschoolers in their attitude toward play.

- There are two types of play: passive (parallel) and interactive (cooperative).

- Interactive play involves both owner and parrot engaging in a mutual activity.

- Passive play consists of owner and parrot engaged in their own separate activities, but in close proximity. This form of play allows the owner to engage in his or her own pursuits—pursuits that the parrot finds interesting to observe and to some degree take a part in.

- Play with one's parrot is limited only by the owner's imagination, the parrot's personality and inclinations, and a concern for its safety.

12

In Conclusion

Hold a true friend with both your hands.

—Kanuri African saying

This book has examined the many ways our friendship with our birds can be strengthened and made more enjoyable. It all starts with sound knowledge of what a parrot is and is not. Corollary to that, we form realistic expectations of its personality and behavior and how these factors shape our relationships with them.

Teaching and drilling the Basic Three Obedience Skills is fundamental to a happy relationship with our birds. Building upon this indispensable foundation, we may add speech training. We may also wish to teach our parrots tricks in order to channel their physical energy and stimulate their considerable intelligence.

We are our parrot's guardians, as well as their friends, and as such, we provide them with safety and security. We supply an excellent diet in order to meet their complex nutritional needs and maintain them on a high health plane. We furnish the emotional love and support tempered with gentle discipline they need to meet their potential as excellent companions. We furnish the enrichment they require to hone their intelligence and keep them free from boredom.

It is no easy or light task to befriend a parrot. It is a responsibility. It is also a joy. I can think of few greater satisfactions than to see a creature of light and air, an individual so different from us yet like us in so many ways, thrive and prosper under our care and devotion to its well-being. When a parrot relaxes on its perch at bedtime, contentedly grinding its beak; when it shakes out its feathers and leans its head trustingly on our chest; when it wags its tail upon seeing our approach; when it confidently preens as it sits quietly on our arm—we know our parrots are happy and at peace with themselves and their world.

It is paradoxical but true that only within discipline—both ours and our birds'—can there be true freedom. In that liberty lies the way truly to enjoy the pleasure of their company.

Index